THE BUDDHIST ESSENE
GOSPEL OF JESUS

A THREE VOLUME EXEGESIS WITH
SYRIAC ARAMAIC TRANSLATIONS UNFOLDING
THE GOSPEL'S MYSTERIES AND UNCOVERING THEIR TRUTH

VOLUME II

The New Age Essene and Maha Bodhi Renaissance

Johnny Lovewisdom

Grateful acknowledgment is made to the following for permission to translate the New Testament Gospel from the original Syriac dialect of Aramaic: The Bible House (British and Foreign Bible Society), The Peshitta Canon, London, December 1919.

Paradisian Publications
San Francisco California USA

First printing 2007

Cover design: Mike Cox, Alpha Advertising

Printed in the United States of America

ISBN-13: 978-0-9725877-2-3
ISBN-10: 0-9725877-2-1

Also by Johnny Lovewisdom

Meditation
Vitalogical Hygiene
Mystical Anthropology
Modern Live Juice Therapy
The Healing Godspell of St. John
Spiritualizing Dietetics: Vitarianism
Maitreya: the Lovewisdom Autobiography
The Lovewisdom Message on Paradise Building
The Ascensional Science of Spiritualizing
Fruitarian Dietetics

CONTENTS

SECOND VOLUME OF THE BUDDHIST ESSENE
GOSPEL OF JESUS

THE NEW AGE ESSENE AND MAHA BODHI RENAISSANCE

THE BUDDHIST ESSENE
GOSPEL OF JESUS

The Origin, The Importance And The Renaissance Of The Maha Bodhi

Siddhartha Buddha, speaking of the Tathagatha Buddhas in the vast preceding ages among his Aryan people shows that in his time people had a record in the erudite sages of tens of thousands of years before him. As I intuitively sought to piece together an immense treasury of ancient legends about prehistoric culture, in my book on "MYSTICAL ANTHROPOLOGY" I began with the frugivorous Paradisian race of my Hyperborean kinfolk in the hoary past of approximately 100,000 years ago in a land of eternal springtime beyond the "north wind". The people were ruled by Boreales or Boreas, so the Greeks tell us, from which their historians derived the name Hyperboreans, or beyond the north wind, just as the northern lights are called aurora borealis. From this aurorean beginning of the cultural paradigm on our planet, we trace man to a sudden loss of his northern Paradise with its surviving inhabitants fleeing to then a forest covered region soon to be lost by the cutting down of the trees to plant grains in what now is called the Gobi desert in northeast Asia. Perhaps the sudden cold which anthropologists say froze mammoths with the grass they were eating still in their mouths, killed the warmth loving tree species also, but like the biblical flood it followed man's deviation from the frugivorous fare of juicy fruits and succulent herbs to the reliance on winter stores of grains and other seasonal crops, animal wool or skins for clothing and ultimately flesh for food.

This only gave impetus for a continuing syndrome from East Turkistan west and southward, to India, Arabia, Mesopotamia, Egypt, Europe and finally in North and South American deserts. We have already shown in the first volume on the Gospel's Divine Mysteries, that A-Brahm is of a rebellious connotation from breaking with Brahminism, coming to Ur of the Chaldeas from the Himalayan mountains to the East, possibly being of a Nazarite Essene Code of Life, if not of direct Buddhist origins. Even the later Essenes, like Jesus himself when he went to India, found the Brahmins steadfast in their worship in human and animal sacrifices to redeem evil men from all sin. So when these Essene sages escaped from the Himalayan region in India, as often occurs, they were joined in their exodus by idealists swelling their ranks who sought freedom, but without the will and heart-felt impetus for steadfast practice. These escapists, like the numerous strict fruitarians that have joined me over the years, but in months or years, soon fell back to their old habits of flesh-eating and other worldly behavior.

This same pattern made for continuance of the cult of Vicarious Atonement among the Jewish invaders of Palestine and Egypt, in spite of having Essene pioneers leading them who held fast to their legend of Paradise in Genesis. Likewise, when the Aryan tribes first invaded India (Carbon 14 dating of about 3,000 B.C.) coming from North Central Asia, they too were come-along turn-coats who were originally inspired by prehistoric Tathagatha Buddhist teachings, but when their pioneering efforts grew difficult, they too had wearied and fell to violence and the evil ways of bestial survival as earth-born sensual men.

In those Mystical Anthropology investigations we tell of the Greeks claiming the Hyperboreans had only one eye, were hairless and nimble like goats. Dr. Howard of Yale has shown that one in 40,000 births is a cyclop with one eye in the middle of the forehead, a throw-back in genes from the ancient origins of man. Soviet scientists have found artifacts in the Lake Baikal region and elsewhere in Siberia depicting this "Eye of Siva", beside Siva in the Lotus Pose and Tantricism existed there many thousands of years ago, altho these same Siva statues, Tantricism, modern domestic conveniences, four wheel carts, canals, water closets, etc. were found among the Indus valley immigrants. Herodotus doubted what the Hyperboreans affirmed about the earth being a sphere, and the Pythagoreans and Tantricism claimed the same thing, so here we have another reason why Buddha's teaching originated in such beginnings. They all go back to the frugivorous Hyperboreans in their former Tathagatha Buddha's teachings of Yoga long before Siddhartha in the sixth century B.C.

Yet among these Aryans which in Buddha's use of the word to mean a holy or divine race, came a hoard of escapists, herding cattle, plundering their resources traveling south to India and Europe famed as the Aryans in an ironical twist of their noble origin. Already in Issedon, those who told Herodotus about the neighboring Hyperboreans before them, the people adopted the cult of the sacrificial lamb mixed with human flesh eaten when a father died. But wherever gold is to be found, a lot of sand must be panned out, or a lot of quartz crushed, to obtain it. To find large numbers of vegetarians, one has to search in great meat-packing regions of Australia, Argentina, in regions around Chicago, etc. Suffering and error like a sculptor's chisel carves out the true and perfect work of art in cultural mastery. We have long, suspected that the ancient sciences of Yoga, Vedanta oriented principles and ancient wisdom now accredited to Hindu Brahmins, have been assimilated from Buddhist antiquity of unwritten or recorded but lost past of the mentioned Tathagathas long before.

"Go ye, O Bhikkhus, and wander forth for the gain of the many, for

the welfare of the many, in compassion for the world, for the good,

for the gain, for the welfare of gods and men. Proclaim, O Bhikkhus,

the Doctrine glorious, preach ye a life of holiness, perfect and pure."

-MAHAVAGGA, VINAYA PITAKA

India's claim as the teacher of the world is due to Buddha. Buddha was born in India and gained enlightenment on India soil. We in the west owe so much to Buddha according to Prof. D.C. Ahir. Universities as great centers of learning first came into existence during the golden age of Buddhism in India from the time of the Buddha (6th century b.c.) to the 7th century a.d., about 1200 years. Our concept of libraries was first developed in these prestigious Buddhist Universities. Democracy can be traced back to Buddhism and how the Sanghas or communities were governed by voting. Buddhist art at Ajanta inspired all of Asia. Indian scholars have pointed out that Patanjali's yoga sutras are really a Hindu version of Buddhist yoga and the Bhagavad Gita is claimed a post-Buddha scripture. Shankara's Vedanta system has been shown to be largely borrowed from Buddhism according to Dr. Das Gupta. The Buddha influenced India to become largely vegetarian after being a heavy beef-eating country.

Your editor's conclusion is that given the same vicarious atonement animal sacrifices, slavery among men and intellectual authoritarian servitude to Brahmanism at the time of the Buddha, -the teachings of Jesus Christ would have converted the world to peace instead of war, vegetarianism instead of high flesh-consumption, and all the democratic principles rather than hypocritical contradictions that western people live with now, and have done so 17 centuries, -had the Essenes been allowed to carry forth the teaching in the West, instead of having been banned by the organized church and religion united under Roman Imperialism. So let us see what the modern Liberator of India has bravely to say in Mahatma Gandhi's address to the Maha Bodhi Society in May 1925:

"I make bold to say that Buddha was not an atheist. God refused to see any person, any devotee who goes in with pride. He made out for Himself an imperishable name. He lives today in the lives of millions of human beings. May God help us realize the message that the Lord Buddha delivered to mankind many hundreds of years ago and may each one of us endeavor to translate that message in our lives..." And when Gandhi was in prison he wrote to the Maha Bodhi editor, "One of the many things for which I revere the life of Gautama Buddha is his utter abolition of untouchability, that is, distinction between high and low."

The founder of the Maha Bodhi Society and journal was Anagarika Dharmapala, born 17th of September 1864 at Colombo Ceylon. Under British rule he was compelled to take on a Christian name, beginning his education under Catholic teachers. When he began to question the lack of moral discipline of Christians who killed man and beast, got drunk, etc., and attacked Christian hypocrisy, he was threatened by expulsion from school, and soon left. Learning of the Theosophical Society, he found solace with Madame Blavatsky and Col. Olcott who then were visiting Ceylon and enabled return of freedom to follow Buddhism which had been banned. Going to India with Mdme. Blavatsky he got momentarily side tracked by teaching of Theosophic cult of the Master but after making pilgrimages to Buddhist shrines at Isipatana, Benares and Buddha Gaya in 1891 and seeing the ruinous state of such holy places, Anagarika Dharmapala, decided his life work should be the revival of Buddhism. At the World Parliament of Religions in 1893 in Chicago U.S.A., he came to represent Buddhism, along with Swami Vivekananda representing Vedanta from India, beside other later tours of the United States, London, etc. in behalf of the Maha Bodhi Society.

Maha Karuna and Maha Bodhi are to be interpreted as the Great Compassion and the Great Wisdom by which the teaching of the Buddha places His religion with indisputable distinction and leadership. On this basis alone wherever one looks among the racial cultures of mankind we can determine the early upbringing of this teaching and teacher. The western mind for long ages held to the theory that cultural civilization began in Asia and traveled west to Europe and America, but this has been completely unfounded by discoveries of high cultural developments in America, before Europe and perhaps even before Christ.

Noting the sharing of plants among South American and Southeast Asian species, does not prove that their conveyors were Buddhist missionaries as we must now do. Thus, it is by the cultural foundation that pre-Inca cultural development points directly to the supremacy of Compassion and Wisdom of the Buddha's global conquest. In effect by the time of the second century before Christ, when Asoka was King of India, there came a dominion of man's environment, an advanced social organization, great architectural advances, hydraulic engineering with great irrigation distribution, manufacture of fine textiles, ceramics, networks of roads, etc. not only in India and Asia, but also in the far-off South American Andes mountains. Prescott and John Collier have described this admirable wisdom and principles that continued two millenniums to the time of the Incas. No one suffered lack of food or clothing and shelter. Their economy was scientifically planned for 20 million inhabitants. Everyone worked but not excessively and was provided for equally, giving a peaceful, industrious and moral behavior. The only identical description of like ways were found in Buddhist and Essene oriented communities.

The Inca people showed a most extraordinary advancement over their European conquerors in social economies. As John Collier wrote: "Maximum human use of land and water with total conservation was the dominant long range policy of the Incas. This is their living, increasing meaning to the world." Abraham Arias Larreta adds potential in speaking of this uniqueness, "The Incas possessed a singular cosmo-vision and philosophy of life clearly differentiated from other people of the continent... The Inca mythology begins with a peaceful genesis, its religion embraces heart-felt cosmovisions and man enjoys philosophical optimism of life... There was not the obsession for torture of Aztec poets, for transitoriness of life and the puzzle of what is beyond in the land of the disincarnate. No Inca poems were ever found exalting the sacrifice of warriors, the glory of immolations in the field of battle, the advance of the heroes to finding death." In repeated ways he shows the superiority of the Incas to other American people, in contrast to European religious wars and modern conflicts we might add. Truly, western culture has been established on the Hebrew-Christian church doctrines about the Savior shedding his blood for us, the martyrdom of holy men, beside secular state education of each nation's history of famous battles and military heroes. In fact, anyone preaching peace and brotherly love among all men is looked upon as a coward, traitor or belonging to a fanatic religious sect.

When Pedro Pizarro inquired about the ruling Incas he found that these tall, long skull people with white skin like that of the Spaniards were descendants of the Viracochas. The long eared Viracochas were a divine race, and they transported and raised colossal blocks and statues weighing over a 700 tons at the ruin sites of Tiahuanico. Disregarding the later adoption by a certain Inca of the name "Viracocha", literally the word means "Who travel upon the ocean like foam, Apu Kon Tiki Viracocha" meaning the supreme god of land, fire and water, uncreated Creator of man and the world. This ancient foundation, Lord and Instructor of the world goes back beyond time and beyond memory, and the coming of the Spanish Conquistadors, was mistaken for the return of the Aryan white men with red hair, whose teacher, the Buddha, wore his chestnut red hair in a top-notch or bun on the top of his head. The unique statues with long-ears and red stone top-notches obviously represent the top-notch mature wisdom and compassion of the Buddha.

The sea-foam meant the white Aryan Buddhist teachers came as missionaries from northern India traveling across the Pacific ocean. Thor Heyerdahl found the stone, long-ear statues on Easter Isle and across the Pacific, altho he failed to realize they came from Asia to America, rather than the reverse as he claimed.

The anthropologist, Robert Suggs observed in "The Island Civilizations of Polynesia", "Between approximately 1800 and 200 B.C. the greatest part of the Pacific had been spanned by swift-sailing double canoes while the contemporary culture of the Mediterranean and Near East were still regarding as major undertakings their relatively short voyages along the coasts of Mediterranean and Indian Ocean." He greatly doubts Heyerdahl's theories as unscientific, but we found Suggs in harmony with idea of missionary attempts of Buddhists from across the Pacific as responsible for the bringing of food plants like the sweet potato from Asia to America, beside art forms of the lotus, the foliated cross, cross-legged figures and other things reminiscent of Buddhist architecture. Abraham Fornander, working as a judge in Hawaii, claimed conclusive proof that the Polynesians were of Cushitic people of Aryan stock who originated in N.W. India and Persia. Like many have said the Polynesians surpassed in seafaring abilities the later hardy Norsemen Vikings.

Another traditional Buddhist teaching observed in the Andes is vegetarianism, which various authors attribute to Pre-Inca people. It is a fact that they had no beasts of burden, raised no live stock, and even when I arrived in Ecuador in 1940, I found they were practically vegetarians, and when they raised animals (sheep, cattle or other kind) it was to sell to Spanish descendants who brought them. Human sacrifice was never found among the Incas, altho found elsewhere in America. Without killing animals men soon stop human violence and war. In the changeover from the pre-Inca Viracochas to the worship of the Son of the Sun of the sun, and the Inca, this still honors the specially Illumined or Enlightened One, much like the Dalai Lama of Tibet represents the incarnation of the Buddha, altho in the Andes actual historical description has been destroyed or lost. The Buddha discouraged discriminating intellectual studies to cultivate the intuitional wisdom. The bulk of what we learn in school is superfluous and has little use in later life, education beginning at home with parents, working the land and gaining a livelihood. The horrors of slavery and degradation of American aborigines brought by the Conquistadors and their Catholic Inquisition authorities has no comparison elsewhere.

Calvin Kephart in his anthropological work on "The Races of Mankind, Their Origin and Migrations," traces a part of the Turanian South American people to having come from Asia, moving across the South Pacific during the peak of the Bubl glacial advance, when the islands formed a land bridge far more conspicuous than it is today, owing to the low level of the water in the ocean due to the evaporation to form glaciers. Larger island areas that then existed shrunk by erosion from continual wave action. Thus we have an alternate theory to prove our thesis.

Dr. Kephart continues, "For example in the region of southern Peru and the Chilean coast there are today certain tribes of primitive origin including Aymara and other Quichua people, of whom the Incas were the most predominant nation. They are quite broad nosed and seemingly represent the Veddas of Ceylon and Papuans." The famous Gateway of the Sun and huge monoliths of Tiahuanaco on route to lake Titicaca to La Paz, denote a high civilization of great antiquity dating back perhaps 10,000 years estimated by Prof. R. Muller, the German scholar. Kephart adds "Only recently scientists have discovered carved symbols supposed to be writing and statues on Easter island that resemble the inscriptions and figures found at Mohenjaro-Daro in the Indus valley of India-and Mesopotamia." In turn, telling of Jesus, Dr. Kephart's reconstructive theory was, "During this intervening period of about 16 years, he apparently at the expense of his grandfather Elijah must have wandered over Persia and India, probably with two Essenes, to acquire the wisdom of the Magi and other Eastern philosophers, for some of his teachings show a striking similarity with the utterances of Gotama Buddha." As to the world being spherical, Kephart says Herodotus disdained such beliefs that were held by the Hyperboreans who bordered the Arctic. So it was probably because Turanians of South America came there due to their lack of fear of dropping off the earth's edge in venturing out across the Pacific, that they migrated east to west, while the other races were sure footed on land only to the west, until the Vikings directed by Finnish Turanians traveled to America, followed by Columbus.

In the first volume we showed that the first book printed in the west, the Gutenburg Bible of 1454, included a figure of a Bodhisattva monk. The fact that this figure came from a carved wood block print shows it must have come from the Far East which is attributable to printing already developed centuries before this among Buddhist monks in China. The Venetian traveller, Marco Polo (1254-1324) brought back fantastic reports on Life in the Far East, Mongolia and China. Beside the use of gunpowder for making fireworks for celebrations, which Europeans adapted to evil use making guns and explosives for war and killing, also he introduced the use of the mariner's compass, and most important, the idea of the printing press which the west adapted not only to pictures, but movable type. The Latin version of the life of Marco Polo was published about 1310, and with a desire to contribute to the production of the first book, the Latin Bible, Marco Polo could well have given the actually used block in use by Buddhist publishers given to him when he returned west. Since no Christian wood block art had been developed adaptable to a press, the momentary need had thus made the use of Far Eastern block with the Bodhisattva illustration with the robe fastened over the shoulder, shaved head and in the gesture of preaching the Dharma, imperative. However the first printed book in the world was the Diamond Sutra of the Buddha completed in 868 A.D. Engraved seals were already used at least by the 3rd century B.C., and Soviet archeologists have proven engraved seals were in use in Southeast Siberia already by 20,000 B.C. So in conclusion, even the first Bible of Christians, and its popularity thru free or inexpensive evangelical distribution, owe their existence to the original predominance of Buddha's teachings.

In "Buddhism in its Relationship with Hinduism" 1891, Anagarika Hewvaitarana Dharmapala describes the Buddhist path (the capitals are the editors), "THE MIDDLE PATH: What did the Tathagatha Buddha promulgate as the basic doctrines of Buddhism? The Four Noble Truths and the Eightfold path. He began: 'There are two extremes, O Bhikshus, the one of sensuality, and the other of asceticism. The one low, ignoble, sensual, unworthy and unprofitable for the attainment of spiritual happiness; the other painful, unworthy and unprofitable. There is a middle Path (Majjhima Patipada) discovered by the Tathagatha, a path which leads to peace of mind, to the (higher wisdom) to full enlightenment, to Nirvana.' THE FOUR-FOLD PATH: For the first time in the history of the world, the Buddha proclaimed a salvation, which each man could gain for himself and by himself in this world during this life. Without the least help from a personal God or Gods, he strongly inculcated the doctrines of self-reliance, of purity, of courtesy, of enlightenment, of peace and of universal love.

Noble Truths that He promulgated were:

1. Corporal Existence is misery.

2. Desire is the producing cause of sorrow.

3. Happiness consists in the extinction of all egoistic desires.

4. The way to get that happiness lies in the Noble Eightfold Path.

THE EIGHT-FOLD PATH: To emancipate himself, he has to tread the Noble Eightfold Path viz.:

1. Samyak Drishti: He has to believe the Law of Moral Retribution (Karma) that every cause has its corresponding effect; and the Law of Reincarnation.

2. Samyak Sankalpana: Leading a religious life in the forgetfulness of Self, and benefiting Humanity and loving all beings as one's self.

3. Samyak Vacana: Speaking truth regardless of consequences; to abstain from slander, abusive language, vain and idle talk.

4. Samyak Karmanta: Abstention from taking life, stealing, committing adultery and taking intoxicating liquors.

5. Samyak Ajiva: Avoiding vicious professions, dealing in murderous weapons, poisons, flesh of animals and human beings.

6. Samyak Vyayama: To engender good thoughts, deeds and words, and to develop and foster them. To extinguish bad thoughts, etc. already developed. To abstain from engendering them.

7. Samyak Sali: Right thoughts consist in meditating upon the impermanence of matter, of sensations, of volition, of the mind, and keeping the mind free from impure thoughts.

8. Samyak Samadhi: Right concentration of the thinking principle.

This is the goal of Buddhists."

The Buddhist path of highest spirituality was open to women equally with man in ancient Buddhist India.

The Buddha may be known for wisdom and highest knowledge but he also was known for great love and compassion. When he saw a dying bird shot by an arrow he was overcome with pain and stunned to silence. When he saw a lamb about to be sacrificed he offered his own life instead. Buddha remained silent when asked about the existence of God because he believed intellectual and philosophical ideas were silenced by perfectness of intuition and first hand experience. His silence said that his self was spread-out in the fullness of creation. How can we hurt sentient creatures human and animal when we feel our own self present in them. His advice to students was Be Your Own Lamp and thus his silence was telling the questioner to discover the fullness of light everywhere present. This discovery is beyond the intellect, the small self or the ego. This supreme knowing that we are everywhere present, naturally makes us flow out with supreme love.

COMMENTARY ON THE UNKNOWN LIFE OF JESUS CHRIST

Your editor discarded the idea of including the "Unknown Life of Jesus Christ" in this work because it only exploits the credulity of the public seeking an Eastern source to the teachings of Jesus, but for the few exceptions of a few similarities, the teaching turned out to be the Hebrew merchants own review of ancestral laws modified by his personal explanation. Instead of Jesus' Essene Gnostic teaching of the ideal of celibate lives being required for the Kingdom of God, the biographers are greatly concerned with Jewish traditions of the necessity of propagating families, having wives and glorifying motherhood as the perfect joy in living, women and wives being the perfect temple of God. Almost nothing is said about the Essene laws of abstinence from alcoholic beverages and the eating of animal flesh. The entire first part is dedicated to the orthodox ideology of the Laws of Moses and Jewish history. A great part of the thesis is dedicated to the teachings of the Brahmins of India, and the Zoroastrians of Persia, with an absence of anything about Buddhism, the object of the whole exposition. Jesus studies at the Buddhist Monastery in Nepal having learned Pali to be able to read the sacred scrolls and then was chosen to spread the Word of Buddha in the land of Israel.

So we end up with an embarrassing humiliation as to what the Word of Buddha was. Perhaps the paucity of information obtained from the Jewish traders, and Notovitch's rendering of the translation, has one overwhelming advantage to make it worth our perusal, which is that it gives it a seal of authenticity! No one, neither the Christians nor the Buddhists, neither Notovitch nor the Jewish traders gained anything from the curious story related, to give them motive to invent or falsify facts that are given. If any party, it was the Ben-Israeli (the sons of Israel) who were numerous in Cashmere. Moreover it presents an orientation which seeks to remove the Jewish blame of what the priests and elders instigated in the crucifixion of the Zealot political Messiah, which had a certain appearance of justice due his criminal behavior, altho it heaped the blame on Pilate and Romans who were trying to maintain law and order.

Aside from the above criticism, the Buddhist scriptures themselves say that 500 years after the Buddha Sakya Muni, another Buddha shall come who shall be known as Maitreya. This scripture seems to be valued on that merit: "Six years later, Issa, whom the Buddha had chosen to spread his holy word, could perfectly explain the scrolls." Just as the novel and motion picture "Around the World in Eighty Days" portrayed, human sacrifices were still practiced in the 19th century by the Brahmins as the manuscript describes of the white priests in India. Placing the blame of the crucifixion on the Roman governor, comes not contrary to the creed of the Roman Church which states, ... "suffered under Pontius Pilate, was crucified, died and was buried", altho their gospels show the priests forced him to do it.

After the Turko-Russian War, Nicolas Notovitch began his travels in Asia, and in 1887 arrived in India, and while visiting the valley of Cashmere learned of the manuscript about the early life of Jesus Christ in India, Nepal and Persia. On October 14th, 1887 he traveled by train to Rawal-Pindi, from there having to travel by two-wheel cart to the end of the Punjab Valley. He then goes on to Jehlun, and Horis to arrive at Srinagar after crossing a lake by boat relieving him from the fatigous trip, contemplating the wondrous scenery of the Cashmere Valley. However, Notovitch makes no mention of so-called Issa's later life at Srinagar and being buried there, missing a vital point to the Christian story.

Then, following the Sindh he travels to Haiena, Granderbal and Kangan. This part is famous for its inhospitable habitants and one of his carriers with a cask of wine for his trip was attacked and killed by a beautiful panther, which escaped before it could be shot. Notovich certainly was not a Buddhist or an Essene in his behavior since he used the whip or bribery to get what he wanted. He boasts of his ability to jump from his horse, to shoot a mother black bear, and then seeing a young cub by its dead mother, he shot it also, and seemed to pride in such things. .

He continues travel from Dras to Kargil, and from there they enter Ladak, sometimes called Little Tibet. Here he notes a great change: "I was treading on Buddhist soil. The inhabitants in this part of the country are of the most simple and gentle character, seemingly ignorant of quarreling at home." Women are scarce, so polyandry (many husbands) is practiced. Near Wakkha he visited a Buddhist Monastery. While drinking tchang, Notovitch asks about a mention of a Dalai Lama of Christians, and was he the Son of God? The chief lama replied "The Buddha did indeed incarnate himself with his intelligence in the sacred person of Issa, who without the aid of fire and sword, went forth to propagate our great and true religion throughout the world." Speaking of the terrestrial Dalai Lama, "whom you give the title of the Father of the Church, there lies the great sin; may it be remitted to the sheep that have strayed from the fold into the evil path... Issa is a great prophet, one of the first after the 22 Buddhas, he is greater than any of the Dalai Lamas for he constitutes a part of the spirituality of the Lord."

CELEBRATION OF THE ESSENE MARRIAGE DISAVOWAL

John 2:1-12, 13-16 (already commented in Volume I), 17-25

ON THE THIRD DAY THERE WAS THE CELEBRATION OF THE
MARRIAGE DISAVOWAL RITE IN THE LAND OF HIS
UNVEILING AND THE DOERS OF THE WILL OF THE LIVING
GOD WERE THERE.

AND JESUS AND HIS DISCIPLES WERE ALSO INVITED FOR THE
CELEBRATION. AND WHEN THEY NEEDED WINE, ONE DOING
THE WILL OF THE LIVING GOD PONDERED, THEY HAVE NO
WINE.

JESUS SAID TO THAT ONE, WHAT IS IT TO ME AND TO YOU,
SISTER; MY TURN HAS NOT YET COME. THE ONE DOING THE
WILL OF GOD SAID TO THE ATTENDANTS, WHATEVER HE
TELLS YOU DO IT.

AND THERE WERE SIX STONE PITCHERS PLACED THERE FOR
THE LUSTRATION OF THE JEWS, WHICH COULD HOLD
SEVERAL GALLONS EACH. JESUS SAID TO THEM, FILL THE
PITCHERS WITH LIVING WATER; AND THEY WERE FILLED UP
TO THE BRIM. THEN HE SAID TO THEM, DRAW OUT NOW, AND
BRING IT TO THE CHIEF GUEST OF THE CELEBRATION: AND
THEY BROUGHT IT.

AND WHEN THE CHIEF GUEST TASTED THE WATER THAT HAD
BECOME WINE, HE DID NOT KNOW WHENCE IT HAD COME;
BUT THE ATTENDANTS KNEW, WHO HAD DRAWN THE LIVING
WATER.

THEN THE CHIEF GUEST CALLED THE BRIDEGROOM. AND HE
SAID TO HIM EVERY MAN AT FIRST BRINGS THE BEST WINE;
AND WHEN THEY HAVE DRUNK, THEN THAT WHICH IS THE
WORST; BUT YOU HAVE KEPT THE BEST UNFERMENTED
WINE UNTIL NOW.

THIS IS THE FIRST MIRACLE WHICH THE LIVING GOD
PERFORMED, AT THE DISAVOWAL IN THE UNVEILING, AND HE
SHOWED HIS GLORY, AND HIS DISCIPLES BELIEVED IN HIM.

AFTER THIS HE WENT TO A SMALL VILLAGE TO REST, HE AND

THE DOERS OF THE WILL OF GOD AND HIS DISCIPLES; AND THEY REMAINED THERE A FEW DAYS.

AND THE JEWISH CROSS-OVER WAS NEARING; SO JESUS WENT UP TO JERUSALEM: AND HE FOUND IN THE SANCTUARY THOSE WHO WERE TRAFFICKING IN: OXEN AND SHEEP AND DOVES, AND THE MONEY CHANGERS SITTING.

AND HE MADE A WHIP OF CORD, AND DROVE THEM ALL OUT OF THE TEMPLE, EVEN THE SHEEP AND THE OXEN AND THE MONEYCHANGERS; AND HE THREW OUT THEIR EXCHANGE MONEY, AND UPSET THEIR TRAYS, AND TO THOSE WHO SOLD DOVES HE SAID, TAKE THESE AWAY FROM HERE; DO NOT MAKE MY FATHER'S SANCTUARY INTO A SHAMBLES.

AND THE DISCIPLES REMEMBERED THAT IT WAS WRITTEN, THE ZEAL FOR YOUR HOUSE HAS EATEN ME UP. THE JEWS ANSWERED AND SAID TO HIM, WHAT SIGN DO YOU SHOW US, SEEING THAT YOU DO THESE THINGS? IN ANSWER JESUS SAID TO THEM, TEAR DOWN THIS TEMPLE, AND IN THREE DAYS I WILL RAISE IT UP.

IT TOOK FORTY-SIX YEARS TO BUILD THIS TEMPLE, AND YOU WILL RAISE IT UP IN THREE DAYS? BUT HE SPOKE CONCERNING THE SANCTUARY OF HIS BODY.

WHEN HE ROSE FROM THE DEAD, HIS DISCIPLES REMEMBERED THAT HE HAD SAID THIS; AND THEY BELIEVED THE SCRIPTURES, AND THE WORD WHICH JESUS SPOKE.

NOW WHEN JESUS WAS IN JERUSALEM AT THE FEAST OF THE PASSOVER, A GREAT MANY BELIEVED IN HIM, BECAUSE THEY SAW THE MIRACLES WHICH HE DID, BUT JESUS DID NOT ENTRUST HIMSELF TO THEM, BECAUSE HE KNEW ALL MEN, AND BECAUSE HE HAD NO NEED THAT ANYONE SHOULD BEAR WITNESS CONCERNING MAN, FOR HE HIMSELF KNEW WHAT WAS IN MAN.

In the Mystery of the Wedding of Cana, John has put the most difficult application of allegorical esoteric significations in the first chapters of his Gospel, since the rest of this and other gospels explain the meaning, bit by bit. So at the celebration of the marriage festivity, we find an alarming contradiction by the very place name, Cana, or QaTNA in Syriac, which was located at modern Kefr Kenna, south west of the sea of Galilee. QaTNA is derived from QTE meaning to legally forsake, cut off or disallow and disavow. So what the disciples are celebrating is the oath against marriage, or the vows of celibate continence. Now, "the mother of Jesus was there", which he has interpreted for us to understand as explained in Matthew 12:50, For whoever does the will of my Father in heaven, he is my brother, my sister and my mother," thus alters the meaning to, "the doers of the will of God".

So the "mother", or the doer of the will of God said to YeShUE, "They have no wine." "What is that to me and to you, sister?" This is because Nazarite vows disallow wine in the ordinary sense. So the doer of God's will said to the attendants, whatever he tells you, do it. Jesus said to them, "Fill the stone pitchers with water." When Jesus asks for water, what he means is just as the Living God explains in John 4:10 to the Samaritan woman, "If you only knew the gift of God (or YUHaNaN, John, in meaning), and who is the man who said to you, Give me to drink, you would have asked him, and he would have given you Living Water". So the helpers or disciples immediately fill the stone pitchers holding several gallons each with the living waters freshly squeezed by the wine press, that is MERITA, meaning must of grapes, or new wine, just as the Living God willed for his brethren, sisters and mother.

The six stone pitchers placed there for the purification of the Jews, shows the Living God's will that Essene Jews baptize their bodies with Living Water, and wash their garments (every cell of God's Sanctuary) with the blood of the Grape, as prophesied in Genesis 49:11, which Apocalypse (7:14) calls the "blood of the Lamb" or Prophesied One of Genesis 49:10, reiterating the "marriage feast of the Lamb" (Apoc. 19:7) where the bridegroom is the chief guest and the bride made ready to be vested in the fine linen of the Saints or Essene Nazarenes. When the water that became unfermented wine was tasted it certainty was the best, full of vitamins and enzymes, the spiritual Living Water as explained in the first volume.

Jean Steinmann remarks that "The baptism which John was to give obviously recalls the Essene baptism", but he is puzzled as to his diet (locusts and wild honey) but adds John abstained from strong drink. Finally he concludes like many authors, "Now the Essenes did not drink wine at their meals, but 'tirosh', a name meaning sweet grape juice".

The wine press in Apocalypse 14:20 in the Aramaic version states "The wine press was trodden until juice came out", from the clusters of fully ripe grapes gathered by the angels, while the western bibles say "blood" not explaining that "blood of the grape" is what washes clean the blood of the Expected of nations or the word also used for Lamb. The Living God, YeShUE, certainly was not the master wine-maker of Cana, nor "a wine-bibber and glutton" or a sinner because he associated and even ate at their homes, altho he lived in the Divine Entrancement or God-Spell (original gospel), and thus was attributed with being surcharged!

Now, perhaps it might be well to explain that this "Marriage disavowal" and cleansing the temple in Jerusalem, are not our invention, but were described in the early versions of the Old Testament, Numbers 6, which is described by Rev. G.J.R.Ouseley in his Gospel of the Holy Twelve. "It is worth noting that while the rite terminating of a Nazarite vow is fully described in the popular version, that the making of the vow is entirely omitted, whether by designs or accident, and lost, we have restored it in the original form. The Law of the Nazarite is simple, and it is this that he who desires to make the vow come with two witnesses to the door of the tabernacle bringing his offerings, a turtle dove, or young pigeon, and a food offering of fine flour, mingled with oil and cup of new wine, and the priest shall enquire the days of the vow if for a period, or while he liveth, and he shall let the birds go free, saying, henceforth I renounce the flesh of bird or beast or fish, and the use of dead bodies, and taking the wine of intoxication, he shall cast it at the foot of the altar, saying, Henceforth I renounce wine and strong drinks wherein is drunkenness, no flesh or strong drink shall enter my mouth, but the fruits of the earth which God hath given me. Then the priest saith, 'The Lord hath heard thy vow, and the God of Jacob defend thee,' and he shall invoke the name of the God of Israel over him. The food offering of fine flour shall then be eaten in peace before the Lord, by the man or woman, the priest and those with them." With the inclusion of the Pauline Epistles that say, "Anything that is sold in the shambles, eat, asking no question for conscience sake," and the Jerusalem Pharisee version of the Old Testament, it is obvious that with flesh and wine addicts as teachers controlling publishing, Essene-Nazarite authentic Scriptures were ignored and dropped from their unholy bible. But in Romans (2:15) Paul says even the Gentiles, "Show the work of the law written on their hearts, and their conscience also bears them witness..." In other words, Paul has no conscience nor law in living.

While we are on the subject, let us be ready to apply the Law of the Nazarite in a correct understanding of the Gospel. Jesus, the Living God, the author of Life, Life-Giver and Breath-Giver, did not kill or eat fish, fowl or flesh of animals, not even locusts. He came not by destroying life, but to make live. So what about the repeated "loaves and fishes miracles? This is the companion allegory to the wine from water, miracle told of in this mystery. Thus, he says, "I am the Living Food (bread) because I came down from heaven", and "Unless you eat of the flesh (or body) and drink of the blood of the Son of man, you shall have no life in yourselves." Yet, in Matthew (18:14) he says, "Your Father in heaven does not want one of these little ones should perish," speaking of sheep, clearly illustrating the primitive Nazarene Christians held that it was not God's will that man eat flesh of any kind.

Furthermore, since Living Water and Living Food carry Life-bearing enzymes and vitamins giving us concentrated solar radiations that give us life force, this is what Jesus refers to in speaking of living water and food sent from heaven, as explained in our first volume. As we have illustrated the original words in the Old and New Testaments have been dropped or misinterpreted, so that the Essene Nazarites must restore the true Word of the Living God. However, the Savior went much farther than this by restoring the original Nazarite redemption for all the sentient beings that men were slaughtering for food in their own living temple, the body, and as sacrifice for men's sins, vividly illustrated in the purification of the temple in Jerusalem, releasing the animals and throwing out money gained for trafficking with Life that belongs to the Living God alone. This we already studied in our first volume but now we show how John spoke directly against what Paul taught in relation to eating anything sold in shambles against the will of God. All who live by the sword shall die by the sword also refers to eating. We might add that the Marriage Disavowal took place on the Jordan border of Samaria, not "city of Galilee", this being interpreted "Land of His Unveiling" or illumination. Now, the first day, John, James and Andrew follow the invisible, ineffable Living God with the Unveiling or Illumination of John, and the second day Andrew tells Simon the Son of JONA, meaning dove or Holy Spirit, but called the Living Stone, and he in turn finds Philip and then Nathanael comes. So the third day, the Living God founds a Living Sanctuary or Temple, building his assembly on the foundation of six Living Stone Pitchers, that are filled with Living Water in the way of the lustration of the Essenes, that becomes the Blood and Body of the Living God in Spirit and Truth. Thus, in three days, Jesus, the Living God has built the Sanctuary of the Living God, but in the end of the Gospel we shall see how those who disobey, and do not follow the will of God and His commandments, will in turn raise up a body temple of erring flesh, rather than that of Spirit and Truth. In teaching of the Buddha's Dharma, if we do not achieve Nirvana in the Self-Realization of Divine Wisdom, our continuum of actions shall reincarnate again and again to carry our Karmic Cross, till we truly deny ourselves further suffering of the flesh in the world of illusion thru our own ignorance.

Philo of Alexandria wrote about 20 A.D.: "They were a sect of Jews, and lived in Syria Palestine, over 4,000 in number and called Essaei, because of their saintliness. Worshippers of God, they did not sacrifice animals, regarding a reverent mind as the only true sacrifice. At first they lived in villages and avoided cities in order to escape the contagion of evils rife therein. They pursued agriculture and other peaceful arts; but did not accumulate gold or silver, nor owned mines. No maker of warlike weapons, no hucksters or traders by land or seas, was to be found among them. Least of all were any slaves found among them; for they saw in slavery a violation of the law of nature, which made all men free brethren, one of the other."

Pliny the Elder about 70 A.D. wrote, "The Hessenes live on the W. side of the Dead Sea. A solitary race, and strange above all others in the world. They live without women, renounce sexual love; they eschew money and live among the palm trees. For thousands of ages the race is perpetuated and yet no one is born into it." Some have thought this identifies them with the Qumran monastery where the Dead Sea Scrolls were discovered, altho the content of those Scrolls disagree with the doctrine of the Essenes at times. Writing of the Therapeutae Essene sect, Philo says "this class of men is to be found in many parts of the inhabited world, both Grecian and non-Grecian world sharing in the perfect good. In Egypt there are crowds of them in every province, and especially round Alexandria." However, the Qumran Zadokite text points to a fleshless diet, "Let not a man make himself abominable with any living creature or creeping thing by eating them." However, this does not explain how it was that some of the scrolls were written on animal skins. St. Jerome says of the Essenes, "Those men perpetually abstained from flesh and wine and had acquired the habit of everyday fasting." This Epiphanius confirms: "The Essenes eschewed the flesh of animals."

Matthew 16:13-18, Matthew 21:42, I-Peter 2:4-11

WHEN JESUS CAME TO THE COUNTRY OF CAESAREA OF
PHILIPPI, HE ASKED HIS DISCIPLES SAYING, WHAT DO MEN
SAY CONCERNING ME, THAT I AM MERELY A SON OF MAN?
THEY SAID, THERE ARE SOME WHO SAY JOHN THE BAPTIST,
BUT OTHERS ELIAS, OR ONE OF THE PROPHETS.

HE SAID TO THEM; WHO DO YOU SAY THAT I AM? SIMON THE
STONE PITCHER POTTER ANSWERED AND SAID: YOU ARE
THE CHRIST, THE SON OF THE LIVING GOD. JESUS ANSWERED
AND SAID TO HIM: BLESSED ARE YOU SIMON THE FOLLOWER
OF THE HOLY SPIRIT; FOR FLESH AND BLOOD DID NOT
REVEAL IT TO YOU, BUT MY FATHER IN HEAVEN.

I TELL YOU ALSO THAT YOU ARE A LIVING STONE, AND UPON
THIS STONE I WILL BUILD MY ASSEMBLY; AND THE MOUTH
OF THE ABYSS SHALL NOT SHUT IN ON IT.

HAVE YOU NEVER READ IN THE SCRIPTURE; THE STONE
WHICH THE BUILDERS REJECTED, THE SAME SHALL BECOME
THE CORNERSTONE; THIS WAS FROM THE LORD, AND IT IS A
MARVEL IN YOUR EYES?

THE ONE TO WHOM YOU ARE COMING IS THE LIVING STONE,
WHICH MEN HAVE REJECTED AND YET HE IS CHOSEN AND
PRECIOUS WITH GOD; YOU ALSO, AS LIVING STONES, BUILD
UP YOURSELVES AND BECOME TEMPLES OF THE DIVINE
SPIRIT AND HOLY PRIESTS TO OFFER UP SPIRITUAL
SACRIFICES, ACCEPTABLE TO GOD THRU JESUS CHRIST.

FOR AS IT IS SAID IN THE SCRIPTURES: BEHOLD, I LAY IN
ZION, A CHIEF CORNER-STONE, APPROVED, PRECIOUS; AND
HE THAT BELIEVES ON HIM SHALL NOT BE ASHAMED.

IT IS TO YOU WHO BELIEVE, THEREFORE, THAT THIS HONOR
IS GIVEN; BUT TO THOSE WHO ARE DISOBEDIENT, HE IS A
STUMBLING STONE AND A STONE OF SCANDAL. AND THEY
STUMBLE BECAUSE THEY ARE DISOBEDIENT TO THE WORD
FOR WHICH THEY WERE APPOINTED.

BUT YOU ARE A CHOSEN PEOPLE; MINISTERS TO THE
KINGDOM, A HOLY PEOPLE, AN ASSEMBLE REDEEMED TO

PROCLAIM THE GLORIES OF HIM WHO HAS CALLED YOU OUT
OF DARKNESS TO THIS MARVELOUS LIGHT; YOU IN THE PAST
WERE NOT CONSIDERED A PEOPLE, BUT WHO ARE NOW THE
PEOPLE OF GOD: WHO HAD NOT OBTAINED MERCY, BUT WHO
NOW HAVE MERCY POURED OUT UPON YOU. DEARLY
BELOVED, I BESEECH YOU AS STRANGERS AND PILGRIMS, TO
ABSTAIN FROM THE DESIRE OF FLESH, WHICH WAR AGAINST
LIFE (THE SOUL).

Just before the mystery we are about to explain in Chapter 16 of
Matthew, Jesus had chided the Pharisees and Saducees about wanting
him to produce a miraculous sign to which he only hints by alluding to
the sign of Jonah. Jonah was a prophet of Galilee contrary to the saying
that none came from Galilee, but when Jesus calls someone the "Son of
Jonah" he refers to its meaning, son of the dove, or Son of the Holy
Spirit. Then He gives his disciples another enigmatic parable, "Beware
of the leaven of the Pharisees and of the Saducees." He had so distracted
their minds that they were filled with "loaves and fishes" produced from
the air, but now they remember not because he mentions food, but he
speaks of leaven used in bread. This leads to the present subject of
whether he is John the Baptist or Elias, because John preached against
bread and wine, and as shown in Volume One, John lived like a spirit
without substance making his disciples think of bread, since right after
the Baptism, he had preached, "Not by bread alone shall man live, but
by every Word of God."

However, altho John was illumined on the Jordan at the Paradisian
Fig Gardens of Simon the Stone Pitcher Potter, Simon in turn after his
purifying baptism of Living Water living on figs and other fruits, is
about to experience the descent of the dove, JONA, or the Divine Spirit,
as a God-born follower of the Holy Spirit in the Living God, Jesus. That
two of the pillar Apostles, John and Simon, realize the incarnate
Hypostasis thru the Baptism of the Holy Spirit and Living Water we
witness the multiplication of the assembly of God, showing that this
foundation or corner-stone is of "Living Stone", as this Simon Peter is
identified with in contrast to Simon Peter, "the Stumbling Stone." They
are both attracted by the Holy Spirit, dove or Jonah, but as shown in
Volume One, the stumbling stone, or Zealot, is not born also of Living
Water, among those drawn, but is attached to loaves and fishes beside
fermented wine.

The rest of the quotation from Matthew and I-Peter, has to do with the part of the present book title, as to the Essene Renaissance. Other than the Pharisees and Saducees, beside the Zealots mentioned in the Gospel, the subject matter is attaining status for the Essenes as the chosen people of precious and worthy illumined wisdom fit for leadership which heretofore has been usurped by bigoted Pharisees and Saducees. However, let us now study the high exaltation of Simon's Illumination. An early copyist dropped the "pitcher potter"or maker, in the original Matthew 16:16, and added Jeremiah, so the word-count for the page came out equal to the original, but thus concealed a "key to the kingdom"!

Matthew 17:1-13, John 11:32-46, Matthew 26:6-15

AND AFTER SIX DAYS JESUS TOOK KEPHAS AND YAQUB AND HIS BROTHER YUHaNaN, AND BROUGHT THEM UP TO A HIGH MOUNTAIN. AND JESUS WAS TRANSFIGURED BEFORE THEM, AND HIS FACE SHONE LIKE THE SUN, AHD HIS CLOTHES TUNED WHITE LIKE LIGHT: AND THERE APPEARED TO THEM MOSES AND ELIAS, AS THEY WERE TALKING TO HIM.

AND KEPHAS ANSWERED AND SAID TO JESUS, MY LORD, IT IS BETTER FOR US TO REMAIN HERE; AND IF YOU WISH, WE WILL MAKE THREE SHELTERS, ONE FOR YOU, ONE FOR MOSES, AND ONE FOR ELIAS.

AND WHILE HE WAS SPEAKING, BEHOLD, A BRIGHT CLOUD OVERSHADOWED THEM, AND A VOICE CAME OUT OF THE CLOUD SAYING, THIS IS MY BELOVED SON, THIS DAY HAVE I BEGOTTEN YOU.

WHEN THE DISCIPLES HEARD IT, THEY THREW THEMSELVES ON THEIR FACES AND THEY WERE IN GREAT FEAR: AND YeShUE CAME NEAR THEM AND TOUCHED THEM, AND SAID, ARISE, DO NOT BE AFRAID.

AND THEY RAISED UP THEIR EYES, AND THEY SAW NO MAN, BUT THE LIVING GOD ALONE. AND AS THEY WERE GOING DOWN FROM THE MOUNTAIN, YeShUE COMMANDED THEM, DO NOT SPEAK OF THIS VISION IN THE PRESENCE OF ANYONE, UNTIL THE SON OF MAN HAS RISEN FROM THE DEAD.

AND HIS DISCIPLES ASKED HIM, AND SAID, WHY THEN DO THE SCRIBES SAY THAT ELIAS WILL COME FIRST? YeShUE ANSWERED AND SAID TO THEM; ELIAS WILL COME FIRST, SO THAT EVERYTHING MIGHT BE FULFILLED. BUT I SAY TO YOU, ELIAS HAS ALREADY COME, AND THEY DID NOT KNOW HIM, AND THEY DID TO HIM WHATEVER THEY PLEASED.

THUS ALSO THE SON OF MAN IS BOUND TO SUFFER FROM THEM. THEN THE DISCIPLES UNDERSTOOD THAT WHAT HE HAD TOLD THEM WAS ABOUT JOHN THE BAPTIST.

WHEN MARY CAME WHERE YeShUE WAS, AND SAW HIM, SHE THREW HERSELF AT HIS FEET, AND SAID TO HIM, MY LORD, IF YOU HAD BEEN HERE, MY BROTHER WOULD NOT HAVE DIED. WHEN YeShUE SAW HER WEEPING, AND THE JEWS WEEPING WHO HAD COME TO BE WITH HER, HE WAS MOVED IN HIS SPIRIT, AND WAS GREATLY DISTURBED.

AND HE SAID, WHERE HAVE YOU LAID HIM? THEY SAID TO HIM, OUR LORD, COME AND SEE. AND YeShUE WAS IN TEARS. THE JEWS THEN SAID, LOOK, HOW MUCH HE LOVED HIM!

SOME OF THEM SAID COULD NOT THIS MAN, WHO OPENED THE EYES OF BLIND MEN, HAVE ALSO KEPT THIS MAN FROM DYING?

AS YeShUE WAS DISTURBED IN HIMSELF AND BECAUSE OF THEM, HE CAME TO THE TOMB. THAT TOMB WAS A CAVE, AND A STONE WAS PLACED AT THE ENTRANCE.

YeShUE SAID, TAKE AWAY THIS STONE. MARTHA, THE SISTER OF THE DEAD MAN, SAID TO HIM, MY LORD, BY THIS TIME HE ALREADY STINKS, FOR HE IS DEAD FOUR DAYS. YeShUE SAID TO HER, DID NOT I SAY TO YOU THAT IF YOU BELIEVE, YOU SHALL SEE THE GLORY OF GOD?

SO THEY TOOK AWAY THE STONE. AND YeShUE LIFTED HIS EYES UPWARDS, AND SAID, O FATHER, I THANK YOU FOR YOU HAVE HEARD ME. AND I KNOW THAT YOU ALWAYS HEAR ME; BUT I SAY THESE THINGS JUST BECAUSE THESE PEOPLE STAND AROUND ME, SO THAT THEY MAY BELIEVE THAT YOU HAVE SENT ME.

AND WHEN HE HAD SAID THIS, HE CRIED WITH A LOUD VOICE, SWATHED MAN COME FORTH. AND THE DEAD MAN CAME FORTH, HIS HANDS AND FEET BOUND WITH BANDAGES, AND HIS FACE BOUND WITH A CLOTH. YeShUE SAID TO THEM, UNBIND HIM, AND LET HIM GO.

MANY OF THE JEWS WHO HAD COME TO MARY, WHEN THEY SAW WHAT THE LIVING GOD HAD DONE, BELIEVED IN HIM. AND SOME OF THEM WENT TO THE PHARISEES, AND TOLD THEM EVERYTHING THE LIVING GOD HAD DONE.

AND WHEN JeShUE WAS AT THE FIG GARDENS, AT THE HOUSE OF SIMON THE PITCHER-MAKER, A WOMAN CAME UP TO HIM WITH AN ALABASTER CRUET OF PRECIOUS PERFUME. AND SHE POURED IT UPON THE HEAD OF YeShUE, WHILE HE WAS RECLINING.

WHEN HIS DISCIPLES SAW IT, THEY WERE DISPLEASED, AND SAID, WHY IS THIS LOSS? FOR IT COULD HAVE BEEN SOLD FOR A GREAT DEAL, AND GIVEN TO THE POOR.

BUT YeShUE UNDERSTOOD IT AND SAID TO THEM, WHY ARE YOU TROUBLING THE WOMAN? SHE HAS DONE A GOOD WORK TO ME.

FOR YOU ALWAYS HAVE THE POOR WITH YOU, BUT YOU WILL NOT HAVE ME ALWAYS. BUT THIS ONE WHO POURED THE PERFUME ON MY BODY, DID IT FOR MY BURIAL. AND TRULY I SAY TO YOU, WHEREVER THIS GOSPEL IS PREACHED THRU-OUT THE WORLD, WHAT SHE HAS DONE WILL ALSO BE TOLD AS A MEMORIAL TO HER.

THEN ONE OF THE TWELVE, CALLED JUDAS OF ISCARIOT, WENT TO THE HIGH PRIESTS; AND HE SAID TO THEM, WHAT ARE YOU WILLING TO GIVE ME, AND I WILL DELIVER HIM TO YOU? AND THEY PROMISED HIM THIRTY PIECES OF SILVER.

After the revelation of the last mystery, that "Simon Peter" therein referred to, was really Simon the Stone Pitcher Maker, rather than "Simon the leper of Bethany", because leprosy, leper, pitcher and pitcher-maker or potter, are all written with the same consonants, GRBA, we see why the words KePhA GaRBA mean specifically Stone Pitcher Maker, since Stone Leprosy or Leper is obviously wrong.

Moreover, in Matthew 17:23, the other "Simon Peter" is rebuked as a stumbling stone or block for not thinking things of God but of men, and he is given a prophecy that "he who shall lose his life for my sake shall find it," just as that Simon does after his recovery from the crucifixion.

So the present mystery starts with the three pillar apostles being taken by the Spirit of the Living God up to the snow-capped Mount Hermon, the source of the Jordan (downflow) river that ends in the Dead Sea. In effect, turning the Jordan back to its source, thus becomes the source of Enlightenment for Simon of Bethany, who now is told by a voice from a luminous cloud, "This day have I begotten you", as a Beloved Son of the Living God. They see no man, only feeling the Presence of the Living God touching their hearts.

That the Living God was transfigured in a luminous cloud, the author has also experienced, and before a host of saints and sages he too prostrated himself being transfigured outside his body in the heavens above, just like the scriptural description, but two years before I actually read the New Testament for the first time. The mention of Elias as the return or reincarnation of John, immediately convinced me that I was the present reincarnation of John, the Baptist and Apostle, just as later I acknowledged that I also was Ananda, the cousin of the Buddha, who I had seen also in that heavenly visit at Pujili, Ecuador on 13th of December 1942. After the angelic form of the Holy Spirit, the Buddha in the Lotus posture, and then numerous saints and sages, it finally focused on Jesus Christ, as I consciously contemplated the awesome vision.

Now, in John's Gospel when John is asked if he is the Christ, or Elias, or one of the prophets, he denies being any of these, yet he admits "there is among you one whom you do not know" (Jn. 1:26), and even he did not know him (Jn.1:31). After he sees the Spirit descend upon him and rest on him, he realizes he is the Son of God, and the "Lamb" or expected one of prophecy, and declares he is the Savior "YeShUE" (Jesus) who is the Christ. When asked about John the Baptist, he said the one ahead of him, in his presence and coming after his former self was John the Baptist, who was Elias, and who now tells his disciples not to tell anyone "of this vision in the presence of anyone till the son of man has risen from the dead". So even Herod recognized Jesus as John the Baptist risen from the dead, just as Simon the Living Stone, experiences rebirth in Jesus at the transfiguration on Mt. Hermon, and to "those who received him, to them he gave power to become Sons of God, especially to those who believe in his name, those who are not of

blood, nor of the will of the flesh, nor the will of man, but born of God."
And thus, "The Word became flesh" dwelling among us everytime his
followers realized this holy Presence or Consciousness of God as Sons.
Yet, John, or Simon, or anyone of us who incarnate YeShUE in the flesh,
as the living temple of His Spirit, is not God in the illusory material
manifestation.

However, John the Apostle ignores the synoptic gospel stories about
being cast in prison and being beheaded for the sake of Herod's
unlawful wife. Josephus, whom we accept as Joseph of Ari-Mathea and
Matthew, was born too late to have witnessed the actual gospel events,
so his story of sending John to Machaerus is the garbled version of
Herod imprisoning his former wife in Machaerus, from where she makes
an easy escape, but thus Herod is able to enjoy marriage to unlawful
wife Herodias, while John is confined to his Jordan hermitage.

As we have already shown, John's Gospel, Epistle and Apocalypse
are all based on the book of Genesis, in his Paradisian Essene teaching.
The Transfiguration vision of Simon of Bethany fig-gardens came with
baptismal purification on Living Water which prepared the body as a
Living Temple of God, built with "Living Stone", for the indwelling or
incarnation of the Holy Spirit of Jesus. This evidently had its beginning
with Creation, or as Dr. Landone interprets it, "Within His spiritual
consciousness, God created the heavens and the earth". As Joan
Steinmann's "Saint John the Baptist" puts it, "The Spirit which brooded
over the face of the waters rests on Jesus, and the divine voice of
Creation in the beginning is that of the Father who recognizes in Jesus
his 'beloved son'." Then Steinmann explains, "But Jesus knew that
John's baptism was of Heaven, that it was a divine institution."

This baptism of Living Water, with fruits and vegetables is the very
basis for the Paradisian status of being born of God so the human seed
abides within in continence as John (I-3:9) explains. Jesus explains also
that his authority is derived from the Baptism of John (Mt.21:25) which
all the people regarded as from Heaven. After the living water baptism,
came the baptism of the Divine Spirit, which John says he has received,
and henceforth preaches the Baptism of living water and Spirit. This
"separation of light from darkness links up with God's work of Creation,
described in the first chapters of Genesis" as Steinmann also observes,
and John emphatically points out that as John he was not the Light, but
was only a witness to the Light of the Wisdom or Word of God.

Let us continue explaining the Syriac scripture of this mystery, to reveal the mystery of Lazarus. However, observe that antecedents to the last mystery of John 11, he shows that "Lazarus" is the brother of Martha and Mary of Bethany which in 10:40 John indicates is at the Jordan Crossing. We have explained in Volume One, how the "Jesus" has been omitted as the name of "Barabbas" in Matthew 27, which thus is taken as the Jesus who carried his own cross in John, but in the synoptic gospels is said to be Simon who was crucified due to Cyrenian riot protests as the Zealot. The same omission from Matthew is true of the "Living Stone" to identify the other Simon, now mislabeled as "Peter". So now, John explains the reason for the esoteric allegory by referring to Simon the Living Stone as "Lazarus", LaEZaR, meaning the swathed man and consequently the concealed one, or veiled mystery man. The Living God has already shown favor in naming John, YUHaNaN, the God-Endowed or God's Grace, but now the "Living Stone" Simon, SeMEUN, is honored by what the name means, as the obedient or true listener, which in I-Peter 2:7, the other Simon Peter admits in not being, so as to make him the stumbling stone, until he is crucified and begins to follow Christ.

The Living God held John to be his Beloved Disciple, but here he admits that Jesus also Loved Lazarus, Martha and Mary of Bethany who devotedly dedicated themselves to the Divine God Spell, or gospel message. What happened now is that while Jesus was away in spiritual work, Lazarus also went into a God-Spell experience, or Divine Entrancement, which in the East is called Samadhi. So Jesus is in no hurry to awaken him, allowing him four days of ecstasy, but when he finally decides to go, Thomas says, "Let us also go and die with him." This John did later also at the foot of the cross, "dying with him" when the other Simon was crucified as "Jesus". Martha greatly doubts when he says, "Your brother will rise up", but the Living God says, "I am the Breath-Giver and the Life-Giver", the actual word signification of "I am the Resurrection and the Life", in Aramaic translation. In the Samadhi trance or deep Divine Entrancement, the breath stops so one appears dead, just as your writer has experienced in 1943 living in the jungle, going into ecstatic trance in which breathing and the heart beat ceased to be taken for being dead for a day and a half, so that the people who I lived with were preparing to bury my body.

But this Lazarus has no connection with Luke's story (16:20-31) of a Lazarus laid down at a rich man's door, afflicted with boils, who when he died came to rest in Abraham's bosom. The same may be true with

Luke's story (7:36-50) of a Pharisee named Simon, between Capernaum and Nain, who asked Jesus to sup with him, and a woman, thought to be Mary Magdalena, anoints Jesus with perfume, being claimed to be a great sinner, and thus being forgiven of her sins because she loved much. Many have thought that Mary of Magdala and Mary of Bethany were the same person, but one was a known sinner and the other was a devotee listening to his teaching and was also beloved to Jesus.

In the first volume we quite vehemently attacked some of the ways that the Roman Papacy twisted the gospel of Jesus to gain favor for its Petrine hierarchy. Our belief is that the Epistles of Peter were truly and literally written in Babylon, where there was a large colony of Jews, and not figuratively in Rome, by the Simon who was crucified and later died in Kashmir. Now, we are restoring the faith in the beautiful tradition that Western Christianity was founded on Simon "Peter", but meaning the "Potter" or Stone Pitcher Maker of Bethany, otherwise known as "Lazarus". In our manuscript "The Word Made Flesh Dwelt Among Us" (1990) we told of the Church tradition that Lazarus with Martha and Mary spent their last days in Gaul (France), altho we did not clarify and elucidate our theme as we now do, showing that there were two Simon Peters that resurrected, but only one was crucified as a famous criminal, while the other was said to have been crucified in Rome in the reverse position or inverted, allegorically meaning exalted to be glorified in truth and thus "uncrucified". This, as Peter's Epistle stated, was because he listened and obeyed John's teaching of being purified by Living Water, the grape blood and fruit of his fig gardens at Bethany.

The gospels, the Latin, the Greek, the Syriac and Aramaic recognize the same fundamental teachings in the Gospels, but due to linguistic interpretation in their translation, Christianity is greatly divided against itself, if not at hostile war. Worst of all, ineffable spiritual concepts have no comparison in speech and description since words were built on materialistic phenomena. Like the early Buddhist divisions of Hinayana and Mahayana sects, which today find harmony and tolerance under the Maha Bodhi Renaissance, Christianity ought to forget their differences for a foundation of understanding in the pristine purity of Primitive Christianity's Nazarene Essene teachings of Jesus.

That the Epistle to the Hebrews was written by Apollos, and not as falsely attributed to Paul is seen in the fact that all the other Epistles of Paul begin with the personal self-assertion that they are by "Paul the Apostle", and nowhere in its text does it bear the weakness of

Paulinism. Apollos was an Essene disciple of John the Baptist, long before the canonical gospels were drawn up and the organized Latin Church. Apollos came as a student of Philo Judaeus of Alexandria, and Philo taught the doctrinal basis as to the Logos, the Word or Wisdom of God, which he illustrates as the "Son of God", the proto-type of the heavenly man or image of God, the source of all good and nothing evil. But Philo lived 20 B.C. to 50 A.D. approximately, while John the Apostle wrote his Gospel and other works near the end of the first century, so since Apollos and John were contemporary inhabitants of Ephesus, they may be fellow collaborators in their teaching.

The Epistle to the Hebrews begins with the repeated theme of the baptism of the Holy Spirit witnessed by John, in which a voice from heaven declared, "You are my Son, this day have I begotten you," which Luke cites in earliest gospel and in Acts 13:33, beside being heard from a voice in a luminous cloud on the Mount Hermon transfiguration in the Living Stone mystery. However, the veiled allegories of John's Gospel as to the need to shed the blood of Christ in the Eucharistic sense, the only begotten son, the good shepherd, brotherly love, and other themes of Johannine inspiration, which in the mouth of Paul would be hypocrisy, pharisaical as he claims to be, since he eats and drinks whatever is set before him, could well come from Apollos' hand. Preaching of the New Jerusalem, heavenly city on the high mountain, connecting Zion to Mt. Hermon, the source of the Jordan and familiarity with the pure diet of Philo's Essenes and John's teaching qualify him in the baptismal rebirth in Christ.

That this Epistle was purloined into Paul's Epistles, and taken from Apollos, so as to make it appear that Paul converted the twelve Ephesians who followed Apollos, is attested to by various authors quoted by Jean Steinmann. "From a detailed comparison of Philo's vocabulary and that of the Epistle to the Hebrews, Father Spicq concludes: 'Beside their vocabulary, metaphors, style, method of interpretation and ideas these two writers show a quite extraordinary similarity of thought, work on the same assumption'... On the whole we subscribe to the theory of Menequoz: 'The author of the Epistle to the Hebrews is the converted disciple of Philo'... Wishing to strengthen his case attributing the Epistle, to Apollos, Father Spicq stresses those characteristics which tend to suggest the connection between this person and the preaching of John the Baptist." Thus, the Synoptic naming of "John the Baptist" as if it did not include John the Apostle, seems to make out that even John the Apostle is a follower of the great "Apostle"

Paul's teachings!

So for further clarification we must remember that the Essene Nazarenes, called Ebionites by Origen and Ebionite Nazarenes of Jerome, thus were the Christians of the Trans-Jordan, who were Essene and Jewish Nazarenes who followed the Gospel of Matthew. The Western Latin and Greek Christianity are based on Paul's doctrine of faith alone needed for redemption, but like James taught that "Faith without works is dead", the author of the Epistle to the Hebrews states that only "the righteous live by my faith,- for whom the Lord loves, he chastens... It is a fearful thing to fall into the hands of the Living God...having our hearts sprinkled and cleansed of evil thoughts and our thoughts washed with the purest water." (10:22, 31,38;12:6)

TRULY, TRULY, I SAY UNTO YOU, HE WHO DOES NOT ENTER BY THE DOOR INTO THE SHEEPFOLD, BUT CLIMBS UP FROM ANOTHER PLACE, HE IS A THIEF AND A BANDIT. BUT HE WHO ENTERS BY THE DOOR, HE IS THE PASTOR.

I AM THE GOOD MINISTER, AND I KNOW MY OWN AMD MY OWN KNOW ME. JUST AS MY FATHER KNOWS ME, I KNOW MY FATHER; AND I SET FORTH CHANGE IN MY LIFE FOR THE SAKE OF MY SPONSORS.

I HAVE OTHER SPONSORS ALSO WHICH ARE NOT OF THIS FOLD; THEM ALSO I MUST BRING, AND THEY WILL HEAR MY VOICE; AND ALL THE SPONSORS WILL BECOME ONE FLOCK AND ONE MINISTER.

THE LIVING GOD ANSWERED AND SAID TO THEM, THE HOUR HAS COME THAT THE SON OF MAN SHOULD BE GLORIFIED. TRULY, TRULY, I SAY UNTO YOU, THAT UNLESS THE SEED, OF SIN FALLS DOWN AND DIES IN THE EARTH, IT WILL BE FORSAKEN; BUT IF IT DIES, IT PRODUCES MUCH FRUIT: HE WHO CHERISHES HIS LIFE WILL LOSE IT; AND HE WHO HAS NO CONCERN FOR HIS OWN LIFE IN THIS WORLD WILL KEEP IT UNTO LIFE EVERLASTING.

IF ANY MAN SERVE ME, LET HIM FOLLOW ME; AND WHERE I AM, THERE ALSO WILL MY MINISTER BE; HE WHO SERVES ME, HIM MY FATHER WILL HONOR.

THERE IS NO GREATER LOVE THAN THIS, WHEN A MAN SETS

FORTH CHANGE IN HIS LIFE FOR THE SAKE OF HIS FRIENDS.
YOU ARE MY FRIENDS IF YOU DO EVERYTHING I COMMAND
YOU.

We have already explained in the First Volume how Simon did not
want to enter the fold by the door, or gate, but sought to climb in by
another way. But Jesus tells him, "I am the door, if any man enter by me,
he shall live and he shall come in and go out to his pastorage." Then in
John 12:23-24, we have the puzzling declaration of losing one's life to
have it for life everlasting, but Luke 9:56 declares, "For the Son of Man
did not come to destroy lives, but to save." So the correct interpretation
comes as Lamsa's Aramaic translation has it, "he who has no concern
for his life in this world", when speaking of loving or cherishing the
pleasure of the flesh in this life. Already in John 10:14-16 above we
explained John's message in relation to people, rather than sheep, but
the allegorical meaning of the words, altho spelled the same in Aramaic,
is in the minister changing his life for the sake of his sponsors,
practicing what one preaches. John was not Promoting sheep raising, but
rather fruit production so as to make earth a Paradise again.

As to the man who serves the Living God, he is his minister, pastor
or shepherd, rather than in the sense of servitude, since the Heavenly
Father will surely recompense him everlastingly. Finally in John 15:13-
14, after being told His commandment, that you love one another, just as
the Living God loves us, He puts it inversely, that we are His friends if
we do everything He commands us. Ordinarily, it says, "when a man
lays down his life", but there is a better esoteric understanding with
allegorical alternate meaning, "when a man sets forth to change his life
for the sake of his friends", as to the "No greater love". It was because
John set forth to change his own life without any concern for the
pleasures of his experience, from the beginning, for the love of his
friends in exemplification, that even when he was condemned by those
who envied him, that he was always saved by his innocence. In turn, his
disciple Simon kept on sinning till his evil ways caught up with him, due
to the seed of sin (grain of wheat) in him, so he had to die, lose
continuity of consciousness, buried in the tomb, so he may repent and
change his life in faithfully following the Living God Consciousness.
Set forth, put or placed is an alternative meaning to lay down: NSIP, and
did change, transmute or alter is the alternative for in place of, for of in
behalf of: kHaLePh, which roots in wash, cleanse purify or healed:
kHaL.

Jesus is the Son of the Living God according to the scriptural definition, and since He said, "I and the Father are One," (Jn.10:30) and "It is the Spirit that gives Life; the flesh is of no account", it means He is the Spirit that gives Life to all living things. Thus, He also said, "I am the Way, the Truth and Life" (Jn.14:6) and "I am the Resurrection and Life", (Jn.11:25) There is no article in Aramaic, so "the" eliminated makes a more suitable meaning as to what "Life" is, showing God is the Spirit that gives Life to living things. So when we say Life, it should mean All Life,- vegetable, animal and human. What we wish to bring out is that men and beast are both living things, part of Life or Jesus, the Living God. Jesus speaks of "Your Heavenly Father does not want one of these little ones to be lost" (Mt.18:14), referring to one sheep in a flock of one hundred, and likewise, "Even the hairs of your head are all numbered" (Lk.12:7), showing that cutting the hair or beard destroys what God gives Life. Ecology is today showing that when man destroys trees and plants, he also destroys not only animal life but also his own life on earth.

In other words, all Life is Divine, and Life is the Divination of all Living Things. Great Mystics and Saints have often affirmed that they see God in all living things. Jesus even called living food and living water, vegetables and fruits, a part of His body and blood. Yet, while fruits and vegetables make it known that eating thereof, is necessary for their reproduction, or revivification (resurrection), animals and man are surely protesting against partaking of their life, requiring their slaughter. It is from this insight of Spiritualizing of Life, that we are taught the Divinization of all living things. From this observation, and what we quoted from John in the original Aramaic text, that we may conclude that the Divine Will is the Will to Live in all living creatures. The Living God wills that animals and criminals, the lowly and the sinful, are to be loved and allowed to live. Jesus came for the sinners and to rescue the sheep, the oxen and the doves from slaughter, because He was the scriptural exemplar or the Hypostasis of the Living God.

The above viewpoints are well substantiated in our time as well as all time as taught by the Buddha. Dr. Albert Schweitzer, the renown Noble laureate, late in the 20th century declared: "Ethics has not only to do with mankind, but with the animal creation as well. This is witnessed in the purpose of St. Francis of Assisi. The explanation which applies only to man must be given up. Thus we shall arrive at saying that ethics is, reverence for all life. This is the ethic of Love widened into universality. It is the ethic of Jesus now recognized as a necessity of thought." Just as we have affirmed, "The renewing of Christianity which must come will be a return to the immediacy and intensity of faith of early Christianity. To dare to go back to the original fountainhead and keep alive true Christianity as it came fresh and sweet and clean from the heart of Jesus himself." As to what provoked its corruption Schweitzer says, as we have held in this work, are due to the Christian dogma that "began with St. Paul and that the religion is non-dogmatic."

"The essential element in Christianity as it was preached by Jesus, is this, that it is only thru Love that we can attain to communion with God. All living knowledge of God rests upon this foundation, that we experience Him in our lives as the Will-to-Love... It no longer allows us to concern ourselves only with other human beings. We must behave in exactly the same way towards all living creatures, of whatever kind, whose fate may in some way be our concern. They too are our kith and kin, inasmuch as they too crave happiness, know the meaning of fear and suffering, and dread annihilation." Dr. Schweitzer continues, "Ethics is nothing else than the reverence for life. All spiritual life meets us within natural life. Reverence for life, therefore, is applied to natural life and spiritual life alike. In the parable of Jesus, the shepherd saves not merely the soul of the lost sheep but the whole animal. Only a universal ethic which embraces every living creature can put us in touch with the universe and the Will which is there manifest." In speaking of creatures he refers to their Creator and thus the Divine Will.

THIRD MILLENNIUM REVISION OF THOMIST SUMMA THEOLOGICA

With the beginning of the Third Millennium of Christianity, I would recommend some revisions to acquire a greater harmony and consequent oneness of Western and Eastern Christianity, as to the basic conception of the 13th century Saint Thomas Aquinas's view of Truth of the Catholic Faith, especially as presented in his Summa Contra Gentiles. These basic revisions are based on the original Essene Nazarene esoteric allegorical method of interpretation of the New Testament Bible in its Syriac-Aramaic dialect of the Savior and the Apostles, which either have been altered from the original Scriptures most ancient manuscripts, or as we have herein illustrated, are defined by the present versions by the Word of God so as to have a special meaning in relation to the Scripture. The latter interpretation has to do with such words as Living God, Living Water, Living Stone, Light, Word, Wisdom, etc.

As St. Thomas observes in Book II S.C.G: "A thing approaches to God's likeness the more perfectly as it resembles Him in those things. For this reason then is there distinctions among created things; that being many, they may receive God's likeness more perfectly than by being one... Because no creature can be equal to God, the presence of multiplicity and variety among created things was necessary that a perfect likeness to God be found in them according to their manner of being." Among human beings, Jesus himself spoke of this need of plurality when He said: "For where there are two or three persons gathered together in my name (my Person, Incarnate Son of God) there am I in the midst of them." (Mt.18:20) This is why it was historically incorrect to speak of Jesus Christ as a man born at the beginning of our Era, because history is about physical men as individuals, and not as the multiplicity and variety of One Person Incarnate in many.

Book IV-7:13 makes it plain, "Nothing created can equal God. The Son is equal to the Father: For John (5:18) says, "The Jews sought the more to kill Him, because He did not only break the Sabbath, but also said God was His Father, making Himself equal to God." So actually what John was teaching was that the Son of God, the Christ, was beyond what the Jews looked at, but "among you stands one whom you do not know" (Jn.1:26) since in his appearance in the flesh, he declared "I am not the Christ." When John was lustrating in Bethany at the Jordan Crossing, "He looked at the Living God while He walked and said, Behold the Prophesied One! When he said it, two of his disciples heard it; and they followed Jesus (or the Living God)." As we have said before James, and Andrew were the two witnesses, gathered in His name, where the Living God was in the midst of them. From thereon we hear very little of John himself in the flesh, but rather hear of his testimony of Jesus, the Living God as the Word and Son of God. John was not Jesus, but was the human witness that gave testimony of the Incarnation, in multiplicity and variety of the One Person.

As Thomas further shows that John in saying: "The Word was made flesh" must not be understood as though the Word had been changed into flesh, but that He assumed flesh, so as to dwell with men and appear visibly to them. "That about which one predicates natural properties consequently on the proper nature pertaining to the genus of substance is the Hypostasis and the supposit of that nature. Since they are not distinct and is one about which one predicates things divine and human concerning Christ, one must say Christ is one hypostasis and one supposit of a human and divine nature." (IV-39:2) "When it is taken for

Christ it supposes an uncreate hypostasis, but when it is taken for others it supposes a created hypostasis."

So authors who deny the existence of an individual named Jesus Christ are quite correct, but yet He did assume flesh as John realized in his witness alone and with his disciples, and this spiritual Christ affirms, "Before Abraham was born, I was," (8:58) meaning he was eternal. This is why it is correct to speak of Him as the Living God, since He is forever living or Everlasting Life, and the flesh body that realizes or assumes Him in time and place is only a living temple, subject to birth and decay.

In God, being and understanding are identical, so that God understands Himself. "The very act of understanding is this: the grasping of that which is understood by the intellect; hence even our intellect understanding itself is within itself, not only as identified with itself in its essence, but also as grasped by itself in the act of understanding. God, therefore must be in Himself as the thing understood in him who understands." The last 'him' was not capitalized so it means the human intellect of John understood the Divine Intellect of the Living God, to be able to bear witness to the abstract Word which he realized to give forth his teaching.

Thomas bases his human hypostasis theory rightfully on John: "Now a likeness of one thing existing in another is essentially an exemplar... Therefore the word conceived in the intellect is an image or the exemplar of the substance of the thing understood. Since the Word of God is the image of God it is necessarily the image of God in His Essence." Next continuing to explain this he says "Since He does not know Himself by any species except His own essence, in fact, His very act of understanding is His essence,- the Wisdom of God cannot be a habit, but is God's very Essence. The Son of God is the Word and the Conception of God understanding Himself." Thus what John's Prologue is preaching is the message of the Buddha in His "Self-Realization of Divine Wisdom." Then, as Thomas admits, "Since the Word of God is true God, it is impossible that the Word be changed into flesh." Here the Western translation is at fault, saying, "The Word was made flesh", and as we have shown from the Syriac translation it should say, "The Word was realized by the flesh," or as Thomas puts it "The Word was assumed by the flesh" rather than "became flesh". The Holy Spirit appeared visibly as a dove at the baptism, and later as tongues of fire to the Apostles, but like the Word as to flesh, the Spirit did not become a dove or fire. Also when John saw "Jesus walking", this is a metaphor, just as when Adam and Eve "heard the voice of God, walking in the garden" of Eden, - (Gen.3:8) He appeared visibly in the world but it did not make God or His Son flesh.

"Demonstrative pronouns refer to the person or hypostasis or supposit. But the man called Jesus says about Himself: Before Abraham was made, I was, and I and the Father are one (Jn.8:58;10:30) and several things which clearly pertain to the divinity of the Word. Therefore, the person and hypostasis of the man speaking is plainly the very person of the Word of God." After this Thomas continues saying: "But that man, speaking in His own person, says that He descended from heaven in John (6:51): 'I am the living bread which came down from heaven.' Necessarily, then, the person and hypostasis of that man must be the person of the person of the Word of God. Again, to ascend into heaven plainly belongs to Christ the man who 'was raised up while the disciples looked on,' as Acts (1:9) says." Here Thomas clearly speaks of man as the divine Son, and not as a man of flesh, for then he explains: "But the man Christ in the flesh had His origin in the world, since He had a true, human, earthly body, as was shown. In His soul, as well, He had no being before He was in the world, for He had a true human soul in whose nature there is no being before it is united to the body." This last statement varies slightly with teachings of the doctrine of reincarnation and modern surgery showing the fetus is a sensitive being.

"For, that it belongs to the Word of God to come into the world John the Evangelist clearly shows (1:10-11): 'He was in the world, and the world was made by Him, and the world knew Him not; He came unto His own.' So, the person and hypostasis of the man speaking is the person and hypostasis of the Word of God." With these citations Thomas plainly demonstrates that the man speaking in the flesh is John, the human person or hypostasis of Jesus Christ, the divine Son and Word of God. Moreover, the fact that the Light of the World, Jesus Christ, as the Word of God was the Wisdom of God, a spiritual entity or thing, the world naturally did not know Him. The only thing the Jews witnessed was John who claimed to have witnessed someone in his presence who they could not see or feel. "The Light shines in the darkness (or world) and the darkness does not apprehend it." The world was not aware of Jesus in the presence of John or other Apostles who spoke about feeling His presence.

Now, as we have illustrated, Simon the Stone Potter or Pitcher

Maker of Bethany, or the "Son of Jonas" meaning "the dove" or the
Holy Spirit, who understands the Word of Jesus, and no longer calls Him
John the Baptist or Evangelist, but says, "You are the Christ, the Son of
the Living God." As Thomas says: "The body of Christ was in the first
moment of conception, formed and organized," and identical to the
Person. In turn, Simon the Stone of Stumbling and Trouble as he
describes himself in his Epistle from Babylon, confesses this was due to
his disobedience, and that the spiritual temple or assembly and
priesthood was built with Living Stones, who lived up to the meaning of
Simon, which is one who listens and obeys, and who "believe in Him",
"the chief cornerstone" of our Faith. (I-Peter 2:4-9) The chief
cornerstone of the Faith that was rejected was the Christ the Son of the
Living God, who in the human incarnation was seen in the pillar
Apostles, since the person or hypostasis of the Living God requires
multiplicity and variety for manifestation. However, Western
Christianity rejected the true Living Stone of the Faith when it confused
the identity of the two Simon Peters, and when the chosen and holy
people of the original Nazarite Essenes are thus revealed to be the true
foundation, the Heavenly Ecclesia of the Living God will reign as the
Church triumphant. Even the Roman Church shall be benefited since the
veiled or swathed Simon, or Lazarus, traveled thru Rome with Mary and
Martha going to preach the true Gnostic Nazarene Faith in Gaul or
France. In Peter's Epistle the stumbling stone of trouble confesses
unveiling the true identities of the living stone and dead block of the
Faith, prophesying the coming confession of the Petrine worldly church.

Finally, the Third Pillar Apostle, James, the head bishop of the early
Nazarene Essene Church in Jerusalem, as described by Hegesippus
(second century A.D.) was a lifelong Nazarite, abstained from any food
that came from animals and strong drink, neither shaved nor cut his hair,
never anointed his body with oil or used a public bath, never wore
woolen, only linen garments, performed priestly offices and prayed
constantly in the Temple for forgiveness of his people. When he was
executed by stoning in Jerusalem the word of Isaiah 3 were fulfilled: Let
us take away the Just because he is offensive to us; wherefore they shall
eat the fruit of their doings. As he was being stoned he knelt down and
cried, "I beseech thee, O Lord God and Father, Forgive them, for they
know not what they do." These words are now attributed to Jesus in
Luke 23:34, beside mention of "the Just" as James was called in Acts
7:52. Clearly, James the Just of Jerusalem was the leader of the primitive
Essene Nazarite Church, or the Jacobite Monosophite Orthodox

Apostolic Succession. This was established and vouched by the New Testament, beside explained by Clement of Alexandria who affirmed "Peter, James and John, after the Ascension of the Savior, though they had been preferred by the Lord, did not contend for the honor but chose James the Just bishop of Jerusalem."

Thus in the New Testament, the Epistle of James comes first among the Catholic Epistles, and even before Paul's Epistles in the official Peshitta Eastern Orthodox Bible. Therein James preaches against Paul's Pharisaical hypocrisy, saying "Faith without works is dead," as a warning to all followers of the Lord Jesus Christ, just as we have shown that the Catholic Epistles of Peter and John did also. After Simon Peter, the Galilean Zealot and stumbling stone, showed his wounds in the Upper Room in Jerusalem, and possibly was seen in Galilee, and he may even have been seen eating flesh with the Gentiles in Antioch as described by Paul (altho too early for that) but after that he is last heard about in the New Testament in this Epistle from Babylon. Finally, John in his Apocalypse likewise in a metaphor uses the harlot of Babylon, drunk with the blood of the saints and martyrs of Jesus, the wine of her wrath, showing how Rome would use Peter who wrote from Babylon, and was the disobedient who was crucified, to gain power through Paul's doctrines in a false Apostolic foundation, prophetically in the first century of our Era.

Now, returning to the theme of "Son of Jonas", or spelled JONA in Syriac and meaning a "dove", which John uses to allegorically speak of the baptismal rebirth as "Son of the Holy Spirit", this has multiple interpretations. The Word or Logos and Spirit was used by the Essenes to symbolize divine Wisdom, as Philo of Alexandria states in "Ques Divinarum heres?" (Who is heir to divine things?), and symbolically called a turtle-dove, because Wisdom loves solitude. According to Serapion of Thymius (330 A.D.) and the teachers of the early church, Logos and Spirit were identical, and in the earliest liturgies the Logos and Spirit is represented as having descended and entered the one who became known as Jesus. In the Testament of the Twelve Patriarchs, in Levi, among the apocryphal Old Testament writings left out of our Bibles but honored by the Scriptures of the Essenes, declares these prophetic words that inspired the Christian Evangelists:

"The Heavens shall be opened, And from the temple of glory shall come upon him consecration, With the Father's voice from Abraham to Isaac. And the glory of the Most High shall be uttered over him, And the

Spirit of Understanding and Sanctification shall rest upon him in the water, And the priesthood of the Gentiles shall be multiplied in knowledge upon earth, And Enlightened thru Grace of the Lord. In his priesthood shall sin come to an end, And the lawless shall cease to do evil. And he shall open the gates of paradise, And shall remove the threatening sword against Adam. And he shall give to the saints to eat from the Tree of Life, And the Spirit of Holiness shall be in them." (version of Dr. Charles)

"When the Logos takes a body, it is the Cosmos. The Heavenly Man is crucified in space. But this crucifixion is of no shame, no disgrace; the cross is the symbol of the Heavenly Man of the Universe and the symbol which the wise have chosen for this mystery in the figure of the Heavenly Man with arms outstretched pouring his life, his love and Light into His creatures. He is the source of all good to the universe, the perpetual self-sacrifice. Far lower down in the scale of being there is another crucifixion, when the spirit is incarnated into the plane where there is the male and female, and thus is cut off from the great life and motion of the Pleroma. The spirit in man is no longer consciously in the gran sweep of the Great Breath, the Nirvanic Ocean of Life ....The mother substance is of so marvelous a nature that the Gnostics called it Wisdom herself, the Highest Vesture with which the spirit should be clothed. The robe of glory or power is the highest spiritual body, or principium individuitis, which participates of the divine and human natures. The living symbol of the 'robe' is a circle 'O', with a cross '+' gives the ancient Gnostic, Carmelite-Essene and Buddhist Nirvanic symbol. The Christ or the Heavenly Man of the Heavenly Kingdom of God, Wisdom called Spirit and the workman Soul, while the accuser (Diabolus) and the ruler of the world (body) and Beelzebub is the ruler of demons (Chaos)." The paragraph concluded is most all quoted from "Fragments from a Faith Forgotten" by G.R.S. Mead.

The Logos in this interpretation is the Highest Self or Divine Mind sent by the Father. The cross, life-giving tree and true vine of the Heavenly Man, Logos and Christ sheds forth grape blood which purifies the Divine Mind-born. In the lower aspect, the Logos was made into the Creator of this world of suffering beings, which the Gnostics like Greek philosophy termed Demiurgos, or illusion of the Buddhists, and what Christ unveiled after His Illumination on the Jordan.

In the Acts of John, one of the most famous of Gnostic texts, he says: "I will tell you another glory, brethren, Sometimes when I meant to touch Him I encountered a material, solid body, but other times when I felt him, his substance was immaterial and incorporeal, as if it did not exist at all." He also found that Jesus never left any footprints. "Jesus was not a human being; instead he was a spiritual being who adapted himself to spiritual perception," as Prof. Elaine Pagels explained it in "The Gnostic Gospels".

The Psychoanalyst, C.G. Jung held that all things originate from the depth, the abyss; from the depth emerge Mind and Truth, and from them in turn, the Word (Logos) and Life. It was the Word that brought humanity into being, and Valentine's creation myth, Dr. Jung interprets as a psychological process and an account of the origin of human consciousness.

In the Apocryphon of John we find, "Immediately the heavens opened and the whole creation which is under heaven shown and the world was shaken. I was afraid and I saw a Light, a child... While looking he became an old Man. And he changed his form again, becoming like a servant. I saw an image, multiple forms of Light. The Presence spoke saying 'John, John why do you doubt, and why are you afraid? You are not unfamiliar with this form are you? Do not be afraid. I am the one who is within you always...I have come to teach you what is and what was and what will be'."

As we have seen, the Spirit is both Mother and Virgin, the consort of the Heavenly Father. "When did a woman conceive by a woman?" (Gospel of Philip) Virgin Birth refers to the mysterious union of the Father and the Holy Spirit. The Valentines held the world originated when Wisdom, the Mother of All, brought forth out of its own suffering. Like the Buddha, the Gnostics held that ignorance, not sin, is what causes human suffering. Gnosticism and psychotherapy use Self-Knowledge or the "Gnosis" in its original meaning, to liberate humans from suffering. It all goes back to the Self-Realization of Divine Wisdom as the Buddha taught it. As Meister Eckhart says: "In Truth, to know the Father we must be the Son." Clement of Alexandria, Church Father and Gnostic, wrote: "The Logos became man that from man you might learn to become God." The biblic allegories along with other Scriptures have their origin in Ancient Wisdom or the Gnosis concealed in allegorical symbols or metaphors, which too late the world has to discover it has mistaken to be history in the Wisdom of the Gospels.

"The Essene Christ", a Recovery of the Historical Jesus, by Dr. Upton Clary Ewing is a worthy contribution to the Essene Renaissance in the West, honoring as he does Albert Schweitzer among other great teachers of the compassionate life. Yet to our students, he continues in the antiquated concepts of worldly church indoctrination which holds "Jesus" to be a human individual apart from the Apostles who incarnated Him as the hypostasis, beside the recent fad of attributing Jesus' teaching to the Dead Sea Scrolls of Qumran which we consider inferior to the Essenes. However, the Nazarite Essenes existed along the Jordan, on Mount Carmel and in Egypt since the time of the biblic Seth on Mt. Hermon and Moses. John's mission was to represent the Essene Jesus in its original Pristine Paradisian Perfection.

Altho we have quoted Tatian extensively in "The Paradisian God Spell", among other quotations from Dr. Ewing let us add these: "Tatian wrote a book on animals but nothing is known about it. He became a pupil of Justin. There he must have written of Problems which Eusebius knew of from mention of it by Rhodo, an Asian writer. In it Rhodo said, Tatian promised to explain the obscure and hidden parts of the scripture. After the death of Justin, Tatian broke with the church and became a leader of the Encratic sect. Clement of Alexandria mentions another book by Tatian, 'On Perfection according to the Savior.' (Goodspeed) The disclosure that Tatian broke with the Pauline branch of the Christian Church and became a leader of the Encratite Christians who were opposed to war, slavery and the slaughter of animals for food, indicates quite clearly that this evangelist had knowledge of the humane Christ, when he wrote his book 'On Perfection according to the Savior.' Tatian's great work was his Diatessaron...The Syriac version into which he put it had a remarkable success, becoming the first Christian scripture of the Syriac speaking Christians. Tatian, with his Syriac Diatessaron seems to have been the founder of Syrian Christianity." Then he tells of Theodoret, bishop of Cyprus who found over 200 copies honored among the churches, which he replaced with the 4 gospel versions. But Dr. Ewing's repetition of church teachings is reversing the process, because Tatian preached from the original single gospel, the original one from which the four canonical Bible Scriptures were versions intended for different churches in the four winds or directions, while the Gnostic gospels were produced for variant ideals or emphasis.

"The Gospel of the Hebrews, or the Gospel as used by the Nazarenes, was called by many the 'authentic Matthew' (authenticum Mattoli Jerome). Eusebius, like Origen, implies that many reckon it Canonical, while the Jewish Christians make use of this Gospel and take small account of others...The original Hebrew Matthew was mentioned by Papia in A.D. 110. Hilgenfeld calls it the 'Punctum Archimedis' of the whole Synoptic problem, taking the place usurped by St. Mark." (Hastings Encyclopedia of Religion)

"The Gospel according to the Apostles was used by the Ebionites. Herein is found the Essene Christ. He denounces sacrifices and the eating of flesh. Jerome identifies this Gospel with the Gospel of the Hebrews. Lipsuis accepts the statement of Jerome and is of the opinion that this Gospel, in the form in which it was known to Epiphanius, Jerome and Origen, was a copy of an older original written in Aramaic." (Hastings Enc.) i.e. the Gospel of the Hebrews, or the true Gospel of Jesus Christ used by the primitive Church. "The Ebionites were a party of Jewish Christians who saw in Jesus a man on whom the Spirit descended at the baptism to fit him for the mission. In practice they were vegetarians, looking with abhorrence on flesh as food and the slaying of animals for sacrifice," (Rev. A. Finlay) "Origen says that those Jews who have received Jesus as Christ are called the Ebionites." (Hastings Enc.)

This gospel used by Ebionites or Nazarenes, Essenes, Hebrews, etc. states "Think not that I came to destroy the law I came to destroy sacrifices, to deliver those that are stumbling to slaughter." (Prov. 24:11) Just as Titus Clemens, one of most learned of early Christian fathers wrote: "Sacrifices were invented by men to be a pretext for eating flesh." This is repeated by Dr. Ewing's writings, quote, "Ye love sacrifice because ye love to eat flesh, but the Lord has no delight in you." Hosea 8:13 R.S.V. actually states "They love sacrifice, they sacrifice flesh and eat it." Dr. Ewing's words are from his "Covenant of Love", a Twentieth Century Gospel of Jesus Christ that does not make, "Jesus into a snare for tons of fish at the command of his voice; to cause a fig tree to wither and die with a barb from his tongue; to make a herd of swine rush madly into the sea with a nod of his head, and to turn gallons of water into barrels of wine with a wave of his hand."

Epiphanius claimed, "The Essenes eschewed the flesh of animals." St. Jerome admired the way of life led by the Essenes saying "Those men who perpetually abstained from eating flesh and wine and had the habit of everyday fasting." The Primitive Christian Church before the 4th century organized rulership of Rome abstained from flesh and wine. The Encyclopedia Britannica states, "The Apostolic Brethren of the Second to the Fourth Century professed an ascetic rigidity of morals. They sought to imitate the manner of life of the Apostles of Christ. They condemned individual property and abstained from wine and flesh meat."

"Papias, the pupil of John the Evangelist, told how John, the disciple of the Lord, related how the Lord would teach that when all creatures would use for food the products of the soil, they would become peaceable and in harmony with one another." (Apostolic Fathers by E.J. Goodspeed) The great exemplar of the merciful Jesus said, "All creatures are created from the same paternal heartbeat of God. Not to hurt our humble brethren is our first duty to them...We have a higher mission. God wishes that we should succor them whenever they require it." (St. Bonaventura) People who live many years without dead animal products become very sensitive to any violation of this purity just as St. Francis confesses in a sermon after a severe illness: "Dearly beloved! I have to confess to God and you that I have eaten cakes made with lard." St. Francis' gift of sympathy seems to have been wider than St. Paul's, for we find no evidence in the great Apostle of a love for nature or for animals. Francis' love of creatures was not simply the offspring of a soft sentimental disposition. It arose from that deep and abiding sense of the presence of God. To him all are from one Father and all are real kin. Francis placed the chief hope of his redemption and the redress of a suffering humanity in the literal imitation of his Divine Master." (Catholic Encyclopedia)

Father Zossima, one of the Franciscan brethren has similar words about realizing the presence of God by loving all creatures: "Love all God's creation. Love every leaf, every ray of God's light. Love the animals, love the plants, love everything. If you love everything, you will perceive the divine mystery of things. And you will come at last to love the whole world with all embracing love. Love the animals: God has given them the rudiments of thought and joy untroubled. Do not trouble it, don't harass them, -don't deprive them of their happiness, don't work against God's intent. Man, do not pride yourself on superiority to the animals: they are without sin, and you with your greatness defile the earth by your appearance on it, and leave traces of your foulness after you... It's all like an ocean, I tell you. Then you would pray to the bird too, consumed by an all-embracing love, in a sort of transport, and pray that they too will forgive you your sin. Treasure this ecstasy, however senseless it may seem to men." (U. Gollcz in Man and God)

Among the followers mentioned in John's first chapter, were Andrew and Philip, both of whom wrote gospels that were used by the Encratites and Apostolic Brethren, being thus Nazarite Essenes who abstain from flesh, wine, strong drink, cutting hair and marriage.

Christians who read the Holy Bible have begun to think that since John's Apocalypse warns anyone who takes away or adds to the book, it applies to the whole Bible. "Do not trust in the lying words of those who say to you, The temple of the Lord, the temple of the Lord. For if you amend your ways and doings, you are the temple of the Lord; if you execute justice between man and his neighbor. Is this house which is called by my name become a den of thieves in your eyes; Behold even I have seen it, says the Lord .... The prophets prophecy falsely and the priests have supported them; and my people love to have it so; and what will you do in the end? .. Lo the lying pen of the scribes has made for falsehood. (Jeremiah 5:31; 7:4,5,11) Jeremiah then clearly shows it is animal slaughter that he is protesting (7:22) "But I brought them out of the land of Egypt, and commanded them not to make sacrifices and to eat flesh."

Theodore Gaster's translation of The Dead Sea Scrolls, likewise protests like the canonical Bible books, saying: "But as for thy people, lying priests flatter them, And the deceitful scribes lead them astray. They have plotted wickedness seeking to exchange Thy Holy engraven word, For smooth things they address to thy people, Making them turn their gaze into the errors they teach, Revel in their feasts, Ensnaring themselves with lusts."

Even the popular Encyclopedia Britannica doubts the truth of the Bible: "There is absolutely no guarantee that the present Pentateuch is in any way identical with the five books which tradition ascribes to Moses, and the necessity for a comprehensive critical investigation of the present contents makes itself felt." In the Clementine Homilies, Peter makes "the rather startling admission that quite a number of the chapters in the Old Testament have been interpolated by the devil."

These Essene accusations of fraud that were made of the Old Testament, may soon be revealed about the New Testament. In the

Eastern Orthodox Aramaic and Syriac versions of the Peshitta, none of the Gospels had any Genealogy from the earliest manuscripts, nor any birth stories as to the Living God, Jesus. When the religion of the Essene Nazarite Jesus was transplanted in Rome by the efforts pioneered by Paul, beside Simon called Lazarus as we have explained, there was no belief in the Virgin Birth of Jesus as the Christ child. But all the pagan gods were born of virgins, and as Justin Martyr's writings show even Plato, Perseus, Hermes, Julius Caesar, Alexander, etc. among the various deified rulers. Thus, Justin concludes as to the current belief that Jesus was born like ordinary men, "even if the majority (of Christians) insist on this opinion and imparted it to me, I cannot cannot agree with them, and will not do so, for by Christ himself we have been commanded to base our conclusions, not on human teachings, but upon predictions set forth by the blessed prophets and imparted in his own teaching."

Thus it was revealed why original Gospel texts were interpolated with the stories of a genealogy and Virgin Birth of the Christ due to the need to comply with the prophecies of the Old Testament and the Son of God revelation of the Jordan Baptism of John. But in the family of Essenes of Joseph, it was known that Mary was with child before she was betrothed to Joseph, and according to the Protevangelion the priests accused him of defiling his virgin before marriage. Joseph was moved to take her against his Nazarite vows due to guidance by an angel of the Lord. Hence the need for the Virgin Birth story. This little stumbling stone took away the Messiahship hopes and deification of Jesus with rumors that he was a bastard of illegitimate birth in attempts to make him even a God of the Roman empire. So this was soon contested with a new book, by James the brother of the Lord, called the Protevangelion. As he told it: "And an angel of the Lord stood by her saying, Fear not Miriam, for thou hast found favor in the eyes of the Lord of all, and thou shalt conceive by his Word. But she on hearing this, reasoned in herself saying, Shall I conceive by the Lord the Living God and yet bear as every woman bears children?" Now Mary was vowed by her parents to know not man all the days of her life, states Syrian Father Ephram.

Also, one must note that James claims to be a brother of the Lord, the God-born, and that MaRIaM conceives by the Word, or Logos in Greek, later identified with the Holy Spirit so as to give spiritual identity, because Logos was to incarnate, rather than father himself!

So with these antecedents, we see the story required making some subtractions in the grandeur of the esoteric spiritual "virgin birth" with Illumination on the Jordan with John's acceptance and experience realized when he was about 30 years of age, lessening the emphasis and switched over to a brief synopsis of an infant born of a Virgin before and after giving birth, now found in the Latin Vulgate and Greek Byzantine versions and genealogies added to Matthew and Luke. However, as we have illustrated the Protevangelion was written, to cover up the identity of John, the Person or Hypostasis who realized the Word as the Son of God, or Jesus Christ, beside to give authority to James and his family relations as leaders or bishops in the early Church in Jerusalem, beside obtain the "son of David" title for Jesus thru his foster father Joseph. Thus came the trip to Bethlehem locating the hiding place of Elizabeth with her infant John, who henceforth are identified as Jesus, virgin born of Mary and her adopted sister Salome among the sons and daughters of the Essene family of Joseph.

Now if we omit the first two chapters of the pre-Jordan Luke as in the Eastern text, the third chapter begins like John's Prologue, ".. The Word of God was realized by John, son of Zacharias in the wilderness"(3:2). But Zacharias was not of Davidic lineage, so thus the lineage from Joseph was added to the third chapter. Altho Elizabeth was barren and thus the virgin birth of John in the aged couple would have been a great miracle for fame, the Davidic lineage prophesies prevented it. Now the 4th verse quoting "The voice of one crying in the wilderness" from Isaiah 40:3, in the Dead Sea scrolls has been interpreted: "Thou hast acted for Thyself and for Thy glory and hast sent among mankind those schooled in Thy council, to the end that they may indeed prepare the way; make straight in the desert a highway for the Lord." In the Mandaic (Nazarene) dialect of Aramaic, Nasuraia and Nasaruta means the Nasorean people schooled and skilled in esoteric knowledge, so here is what was transliterated in Luke 2:4 saying that Joseph also went from Nazareth, or Joseph's Essene School of Enlightenment (GaLILA) not in Galilea, but Na'areth of Samaria by the Jordan.

The weighty evidence of both Mark and John's Gospel in lacking birth stories other than John's rebirth by the Jordan baptism and Simon the Pitcher Maker on Mt. Hermon, beside the facts admitted by Justin that Matthew and Luke manuscripts in his time only spoke of illumination on the Jordan and "This day have I begotten thee", with divine lineage without human seed being born of grape blood, show that Jesus Christ was not the name of a human person at physical birth, but rather..accommodated for the Hypostasis or Person of the Holy Trinity prophesied by ancient Scriptures. Naturally, the linguistic terminology as interpreted by the Eastern and Western Christians thus ran into conflict and split the Church into the Eastern Nestorian, and Orthodox Jacobites, the Byzantine Greek and the Pauline Roman Catholics with their compromise middle ground. The so-called falsifying and interpolating of the canonical Bible was not intended out of mischief but history rebelled against the truth, and Christianity would never have become a predominant religion of a great part of the world if only the pure truth and strict practice of the primitive Nazarite Essene discipline were insisted upon. Thus, our preaching of the new Essene Renaissance, since Christians know the basic Christian concepts for the foundation, so that we may update it in a primitive Aramaic interpretation of Essene truths, and effective practice of religion.

Even more important than the beginning parts of the gospels with birth and lineage interpretations, is latter concluding mysteries of Christ's crucifixion and resurrection stories to be seen in the modern light of religious understanding. Christ dying for our sins is a superstitious belief in incongruent vicarious atonement, and gives motive to "accept Jesus as our Savior", without doing anything more about our own degraded sinful life. Worst of all, it was this point that church leadership has made a political tool for the conscription of armies and the waging of war, inquisition or wars of Christians against Christians beside foreign religions, violating all of God's commandments and human conscience. Jesus preached that one needs to deny himself, take up his Cross which is a Yoke, burden or Karma, and follow Him in practice. If we fail to follow Him, the gospel shows how the disobedient die and will revive till they learn.

Mark 8:31-38, I-John 2:2-6, I-John 4:1-19

AND HE BEGAN TO TEACH THEM THAT THE SON OF MAN MUST SUFFER MANY THINGS, AND BE REJECTED BY THE ELDERS AND THE CHIEF PRIESTS AND SCRIBES, AND BE PUT TO DEATH, AND AFTER THREE DAYS RISE AGAIN.

AND WHAT HE SAID HE SPOKE OPENLY. AND PETER TAKING HIM ASIDE, BEGAN TO CHIDE HIM. BUT HE, TURNING AND SEEING HIS DISCIPLES, REBUKED SIMON, SAYING, GET BEHIND ME SATAN, FOR YOU ARE NOT THINKING THE

THINGS OF GOD, BUT THOSE OF MEN.

AND CALLING THE CROWD TOGETHER WITH THE DISCIPLES, HE SAID TO THEM, IF ANYONE WISHES TO COME AFTER ME, LET HIM DENY HIMSELF, AND TAKE UP HIS CROSS, AND FOLLOW ME. FOR HE WHO WOULD SAVE HIS SELF WILL HAVE TO GIVE IT UP, BUT HE WHO GIVES UP HIS SELF FOR MY SAKE AND THE SAKE OF MY GOSPEL, WILL SAVE IT.

FOR WHAT DOES IT PROFIT A MAN, IF HE GAIN THE WHOLE WORLD, BUT SUFFER THE LOSS OF HIS LIFE? OR WHAT COULD A MAN GIVE IN EXCHANGE FOR HIS LIFE?

FOR WHOEVER IS ASHAMED OF ME AND MY WORD IN THIS ADULTEROUS AND SINFUL GENERATION, OF HIM WILL THE SON OF MAN ALSO BE ASHAMED WHEN HE COMES WITH HIS HOLY ANGELS IN THE GLORY OF HIS FATHER.

AND HE IS A PROPITIATION FOR OUR SINS, AND NOT OF OURS ONLY, BUT FOR THE SINS OF THE WHOLE WORLD. AND BY THIS WE CAN BE SURE THAT WE KNOW HIM, IF WE KEEP HIS COMMANDMENTS.

HE WHO SAYS HE KNOWS HIM; AND DOES NOT KEEP HIS COMMANDMENTS, IS A LIAR AND THE TRUTH IS NOT IN HIM. BUT HE WHO KEEPS HIS WORD, IN HIM THE LOVE OF GOD IS TRULY PERFECTED; HE WHO SAYS THAT HE ABIDES IN HIM, OUGHT HIMSELF ALSO TO WALK JUST AS HE WALKED.

BELOVED, DO NOT BELIEVE EVERY SPIRIT, BUT TEST THE SPIRITS TO SEE WHETHER THEY ARE OF GOD; BECAUSE MANY FALSE PROPHETS HAVE GONE FORTH INTO THE WORLD.

BY THIS IS THE SPIRIT OF GOD KNOWN: EVERY SPIRIT THAT CONFESSES THAT JESUS CHRIST HAS COME IN THE FLESH, IS OF GOD. AND EVERY SPIRIT THAT SEVERS JESUS, IS NOT OF GOD, BUT IS OF THE ANTICHRIST, OF WHOM YOU HAVE HEARD HE IS COMING, AND NOW IS ALREADY HERE.

YOU ARE OF GOD, MY CHILDREN, AND HAVE OVERCOME

THEM, BECAUSE GREATER IS HE WHO IS IN YOU THAN HE
WHO IS IN THE WORLD.

THEY ARE OF THE WORLD; THEREFORE OF THE WORLD THEY
SPEAK AND THE WORLD LISTENS TO THEM. WE ARE OF GOD.
HE KNOWS AND LISTENS TO US; HE WHO IS NOT OF GOD
DOES NOT LISTEN TO US. BY THIS WE KNOW THE SPIRIT OF
TRUTH AND SPIRIT OF ERROR.

BELOVED, LET US LOVE ONE ANOTHER, FOR LOVE IS FROM
GOD. HE WHO DOES NOT LOVE DOES NOT KNOW GOD; FOR
GOD IS LOVE. IN THIS HAS THE LOVE OF GOD BEEN SHOWN
TOWARD US, THAT GOD HAS SENT HIS ONLY BEGOTTEN SON
INTO THE WORLD THAT WE MAY LIVE THROUGH HIM.

IN THIS IS THE LOVE, NOT THAT WE HAVE LOVED GOD, BUT
HE HAS FIRST LOVED US, AND SENT HIS SON A PROPITIATION
FOR OUR SINS. BELOVED, IF GOD SO LOVED US, WE ALSO
OUGHT TO LOVE ONE ANOTHER.

NO ONE HAS EVER SEEN GOD. IF WE LOVE ONE ANOTHER
GOD ABIDES IN US AND HIS LOVE IS PERFECTED IN US. IN
THIS WE KNOW THAT WE ABIDE IN HIM AND HE IN US,
BECAUSE HE HAS GIVEN US OF HIS SPIRIT.

AND WE HAVE SEEN AND DO TESTIFY, THAT THE FATHER HAS
SENT HIS SON TO BE THE SAVIOR OF THE WORLD. WHOEVER
CONFESSES THAT JESUS IS THE SON OF GOD, GOD ABIDES IN
HIM AND HE IN GOD.

AND WE HAVE COME TO KNOW AND HAVE BELIEVED, THE
LOVE THAT GOD HAS IN OUR BEHALF. GOD IS LOVE, AND HE
WHO ABIDES IN LOVE ABIDES IN GOD AND GOD IN HIM.

IN THIS IS LOVE PERFECTED IN US, THAT WE MAY HAVE
CONFIDENCE IN THE DAY OF JUDGEMENT; BECAUSE AS HE IS
EVEN SO ARE WE ALSO IN THIS WORLD.

THERE IS NO FEAR IN LOVE; BUT PERFECT LOVE CASTS OUT
FEAR, BECAUSE FEAR BRINGS FORTH TORMENT. AND HE
WHO FEARS IS NOT PERFECTED IN LOVE. LET US THEREFORE

LOVE, BECAUSE GOD FIRST LOVED US.

THE SON OF MAN WHO SUFFERED, DIED, WAS BURIED AND
ROSE FOR OUR SINS.

In "The Origins of Christianity" Prof. Frederick C. Conybeare of
University College, Oxford, presents a dialogue of the Pillar Apostles,
James, Peter and John, against Paul as to why, "By what right, did Paul
attribute his dreams and fancies to Christ whom he had not known, and
from whom he had never received any apostolic commission? They
scoffed at his revelations, and, in the heat of the conflict, even went so
far as to identify him with the anti-Christ." John goes directly to this
point: "He who says he knows him, and does not keep his
commandments, and is a liar and the truth is not in him... Who is a liar
but he who denies that Jesus is the Christ? He is the Anti-Christ who
denies the Father and the Son... And every spirit that denies that Jesus
Christ is come in the flesh is not of God; and this is the spirit of the anti-
Christ, whereof you have heard he is to come, and who is even now
already in the world." John does not name Paul, but states that he does
not follow the precepts of the Pillar Apostles who came in the flesh
preaching the gospel of the Essene Christ. Anyone who goes around
boldly eating the flesh of animals, meat that is sold in the shambles and
has to be slaughtered requiring its killing, and a consumer of alcoholic
drinks can hardly be trusted to be in his right mind ever.

However, Paul sneers at the exclusive pretensions of the twelve
apostles and falls back on his own visions. He argues he had seen the
Christ and had been commissioned to preach to the Gentiles. As
Conybeare put it, "He is equally silent about moral and religious
teachings of the Master, and shows no acquaintance with the Sermon on
the Mount and with the parables... and is absorbed in his own
hallucinations and transcendental fancies,- grandiose, it is true, but
sorely baffling our modern curiosity." At Antioch, Paul found himself
resisting "Peter to the face," and calls the Pillar Apostles, "false
brethren", "privily brought in to spy out our liberty which we have in
Jesus Christ." Paul's gospel, thus, has nothing to do with the Essenes,
and so, the Essenes were never mentioned in New Testament
Translations, because "For neither did I receive it from man, nor was I
taught it, except by way of revelation on the part of Jesus Christ." Thus,
Paul preached not the historical Jesus, but a messianic conception of his
own, Conybeare elucidated, and concluded, "Paul was aware that his

initial revelation conflicted with the tradition of the earthy Jesus, and for this reason avoided Jerusalem and the apostles that were before him." Paul explains his connection in Corinthians 15 saying: "Christ died for our sins according to the Scriptures; and was buried and that he hath been raised on the third day according to the Scriptures; and he appeared to Cephas; then to the twelve; also he appeared to above five hundred brethren at once, some of which are fallen asleep then he appeared to James; then all the apostles and last of all, as unto one born out of due time, he appeared to me."

So what the Pauline gospel is based on is visionary appearances and thus "severs Jesus Christ came in the flesh and is not of God, but is of the Anti-Christ... now already in the world" as the Catholic version gives I-John 4:3. At Caesarea of Philippi when Peter rebuked Jesus, he answered beginning to teach them, "a son of man will have to suffer a great deal, and be rejected by the elders and the high priests and scribes, and be killed, and rise again the third day." (Mk.8:31) Commenting on this, Conybeare explains, "The Son of Man seems to bear its ordinary Semitic meaning of a human being, man in general; but in the transfiguration episode and thru-out the rest of the Gospel, it bears the meaning aligned to it in the Book of Daniel (some 200 years B.C.) wherein we read as follows; "I saw in the night visions, and behold, there came with the clouds of heaven one like unto a son of man and he came even to the Ancient of days and they brought him before him." (7:13) But Conybeare, like the rest of the Latin Church indoctrinated observers, failed to see that Jesus was in this particular case with Simon, his stumbling stone "Peter", foretelling the suffering, crucifixion and revival of whom Jesus now labels "Satan"; and his dying was due to the self-same sins that all men, man or the son of man suffers and dies for, only to be revived in the same body as Simon was, or rise reincarnating in a new-born body within 3 days of one's death. This doctrine obviously is that of John and his followers, thus propagating Buddhas doctrines in the West esoterically.

However, Oxford's Professor Conybeare did blaze the trail for recovering the Essene Nazarene interpretation of what John in his own time was referring to as to the spirit of the Anti-Christ or false Christ which Paul preached in his Epistles. Going on to Paul's theological theme, he approaches his Jewish compatriots saying,- "Are they Hebrews? So am I. Are they Israelites? So am I. Are they the seed of Abraham? So am I." (II-Cor.11:22) After this he boasts of how he has

been beaten, stoned, imprisoned and shipwrecked more than any other
Christian. More, he says (12:2): "I knew a man in Christ over 14 years
ago but whether I knew him in body or without body, I do not know, God
knows. And I still know this man, but whether in a body or without a
body, I do not know." This is Paul's Christ, of whom he admits he does
not know if it was phantasm or not, and moreover ignors and denies that
his coming in the flesh has any importance.

What remains Jewish in him is his means of approach, boasting of his
hypocritical Phariseeism. Justin Martyr explains according to his friend
Trypho, "We Jews all expect that the Messiah will be a man of purely
human origin. This, then, is the rationale upon which the need of the
Christ to incarnate in the flesh is based. According to Paul's doctrine, the
sins of all mankind are nailed to the cross, but when he rose from the
dead, the risen body was shared by all those redeemed by sheer belief.
And here Paul's sacramental theology built on the pagan mysteries,
comes in.

Paul again boasts, "All things are lawful for me." (I-Cor. 6:12) So all
his boasts of Judaism come to nothing, since he no longer is under the
Law. The Sacramental Union with Jesus puts Christians above the Law,
just as the pagan mysteries obtained salvation with no moral obligation,
by communion with their god. This is just what Pauline Theology comes
to in what it has done for so-called Christianity. Of course he wavers,
uneasy in conscience, saying, "Not all things are expedient", but
expedient or not, this whole approach is what is today observed in
Catholic Latin America especially. By going to Holy Mass they renew
their status as "good Christians", and then they head at once straight for
the bar or liquor store and get drunk, coming home to abuse wife and
children. In Vilcabamba on Sundays, the shambles selling pieces of
animal carcasses was to the right of the church entrance, and on St.
Francis Day the priest gave a sermon promoting the eating of flesh as
higher theology than that of the Saint of Assisi.

This Satanic influence of the Anti-Christ has crept in all over the
world thru missionary preaching, sacramentalism and cheap or free Bible
scriptures. Paul used dishonesty for what he believed a good cause, and
many were the Church Fathers that perpetuated disobedience to Essene
precepts with use of his theology. Paul is "all things to all people", with
the Jews he preaches Jewish doctrine, and with the gentiles he dispenses
with Mosaic Law to make them Israelites. But everywhere he goes, he

finds his lies catching up with him, causing him to be beaten, stoned, imprisoned, etc. It all comes to a head when he was on trial for his life, since he was accused for apostasy of his religion, and a provoker of unrest thru-out the empire. So he appeals "I came to bring Alms to my nation and offer an offering. So these men found me purified in the temple." (Acts 24:18) "I labor to always have a clear conscience before God and before man."

Well, how does this compare with what he tells the Nazarenes in Jerusalem? He tells them he made collections of funds for the Poor, or Ebionites at the chief congregation of the Nazarene Church. So, he disturbs the peace all over the Roman Empire with his trick claim to be a Jew collecting funds for the temple, and likewise ransoming himself collecting funds for the Essene Nazarene congregation of the poor. So Paul has been warned against for preaching division in Christ,-his double-faced doctrine showed him to be a lying crook as every one of the pillar apostles demonstrated in their letters. He teaches against the Mosaic Law and then bribes the temple, and the same with Bishop James to receive the right hand of fellowship, only to turn around and teach that Christians should eat without questioning for conscience sake, flesh from the shambles, or whatever is put before them. (I-Cor. 10:25-27) He was kicked out of Antioch and Ephesus, and stoned and persecuted everywhere because he could not see how greatly paranoid and double faced he was.

James, the head bishop of the Nazarene Church in Jerusalem preached, "Faith without works is dead of itself... You see then how a man by works becomes righteous, and not by faith." (James 2:17,24) Likewise, Peter warns against false prophets and then names Paul (II 3:15-17), "Even our beloved brother Paul, according to wisdom given to him has written in all his Epistles... there are certain things difficult to understand that those who are ignorant and unstable pervert their meaning." As kindly as Peter puts it, he lets him know that his own ignorance and instability will bring Paul "unto his own destruction" in preaching his lawless doctrine. Even if Peter was illiterate and needed others to write his letters, it was well put.

John, as our Syriac translation shows, calls those like Paul liars by saying "He who says, I know him, and does not keep his commandments, is a liar and the truth is not in him." Beside numerous things in his letters that point to Paul as a false Christ, that is, the Anti-Christ, in the

Apocalypse, John refers to him by the pseudo-Gnostic title of "Nicolaitans". Paul was afraid of the Ephesians since these were the followers of the "Christians of St. John" meaning the Gnostic Nazarenes. "This you have in your favor, you hate the works of the Nicolaitans which also I hate." (Apoc.2:6) He adds speaking to the Church at Pergamos, "Balaam who taught Balac to cast a stumbling block before the children of Israel, to eat sacrificed flesh and commit fornication. As also do they who hold to the doctrine of the Nicolaitans". (2:16) NeKOL means crafty, tricky, in the Syriac dialect, while in the Mandaic dialect of Aramaic, NIKLA means deceit. In the Syriac Lexicon it defines NIQLITU as followers of Nicolaus, probably a cryptic designation of Paulinism. Also in the Mandaic dialect MSIHI PAULIS is used to designate those who follow Paul as the Messiah, which John speaks of as Anti-Christ. Mandaic is the Gnostic tongue used by his followers to this day in Mesopotamia.

Particularly interesting is Paul's own details in Galatians telling of when some emissaries, or "spies" of James came to Antioch, and also in Acts 9 and 10 which tell of Peter going to visit the tanner at Joppa and ministering there. Then, in Galatians 2:14 Paul says, "If you being a Jew, live after the manner of the Gentiles and not as do the Jews, why do you compel the Gentile converts to live as do the Jews?" This may be no more than in the case of the disciples eating without washing their hands in Mark 7, so Jesus says what enters a man cannot defile a man, but what comes out of him. So the Bible-correctors took the opportunity to add, "Thus he declared all foods clean," to match Paul's preaching of flesh-eating, which was never in the Eastern Peshitta text, nor ancient gospel manuscripts. Now in Acts 10 and 11 Peter has visions of flesh and killing for food, but after his recovery from the crucifixion when he resolved to live like an Essene, he also gave up flesh foods, and the seeing of visions or dreams about eating meat after starting vegetarianism is a common astral phenomena due to one's habitual desires. All evil habits take years to overcome, and the way to overcome them is to deny, or forsake the self built on our desires, or taking up the crossing out of sin by following Jesus.

In the Palestinian Syriac text illustration of Mark 8:34-36 it says, "If anyone wishes to come after me, let him deny himself, and take up his cross, and follow me. For he who would save his self will have to give it up, but he who gives up his self for my sake and the sake of my Gospel, will save it. For what does it profit a man, if he gain the whole world, but suffer the loss of his life?" Here the problem in translation is the word NaPhShA, which means the vital or animating principle, the soul or the heart, life and self. In relation to Peter, it is prophesying his crucifixion, just as it prophecies the suffering that worldly people go thru when they die, especially if they possess much. However, the deeper esoteric wisdom is seen in how Jesus teaches Buddhist Yoga, in taking up the Yoke (Cross) and disowning one's habitual desires for bodily pleasure, and practicing the higher true Self-Realization in Buddha, or Christ, in selflessness. This uniting in the Living God-Self is the Emancipation from the recurring cycles of birth and death due to not giving up one's worldly desires.

John surnamed Mark, being rejected by Paul, joins his father in his voyage to Babylon, reinforcing Peter's faith, and clearing up the esoteric meaning of what worldly people only see in the gospel, that need of "losing one's life" for salvation and Eternal Life. HIA means live, save, heal, and is the salvation or Eternal Life Jesus the Living God teaches. As we shall show, "No one has ever seen God. (But) If we love one another, God abides in us and his love is perfected in us. In this we know that we abide in him and he in us, because he has given us of his Spirit." Thus, God is experienced within, and no one ever saw a man named Jesus Christ preaching in Palestine. Yet, the very Apostles insist he came, and forever will come even to abide in us. Like the Manichaeans preached, he hung on every fruit tree, he was served up in every living food dish, a palatable Jesus, "living food cast down from heaven", and not slaughtered flesh of the shambles, baked bread and fermented wine, just as John preached about the Living God, Jesus.

John, nor Jesus speaking thru him, was not teaching suicide and destroying the living temple of our bodies with penances and going about provoking one's own martyrdom like Paul practiced because he had never given up his ego and preached his own gospel against the Essenes. This is why we have deliberated at length on this subject of really, giving up or denying the self, and altho life means the same self, it must be explained and understood as such, applying it to our sensual pleasures and worldly desires by which we refer to man's self.

Why were the Nazarene Essenes sure that their doctrine would be understood by the Gentiles being converted to the basic doctrine of abstaining from eating flesh and killing? Why would John write that men would know Jesus Christ come in the flesh if they kept his commandments? The Catholic Epistles followed directly after the Acts of the Apostles, and in Acts 15 this very question had been thrashed out and made clear. Certain Pharisees had insisted that Gentile converts had to be circumcised surgically, a cause that Paul presented to the head Apostles in Jerusalem. The upshot of this question was that those who taught the requirement of circumcision were contradicted, they said "on these things we have never commanded them" (15:24), and finally, "For it is the will of the Holy Spirit and of us, to lay upon you no additional burden than THESE NECESSARY THINGS: THAT YOU ABSTAIN FROM IMMOLATING ANIMALS, BOTH FROM BLEEDING THEM AND FROM STRANGLING THEM, AND FROM FORNICATION: when you keep yourselves from these things, you do well. Remain steadfast in our Lord." So how does this compare with Paul's teaching: "Anything for sale in the shambles, that eat without question for conscience sake: For the earth is the Lord's and the fullness thereof. If any pagan invite you and you wish to go, whatever is set before you eat, without question for conscience sake." (I-Cor.10:25-27) The Christ of Paul is neither an Essene, nor a Pharisee, but a Pagan spirit! As he himself says: "You cannot be partakers of the table of our Lord and of the table of devils." He prefers devil worship!

In chapter 11 of the same epistle Paul even attacks the Nazarite Essene vow against cutting the hair and beard, saying they are a disgrace to a man, showing he has completely broken with the Nazarene-Essene Christians, and founded a new sect of Pauline Christianity. The abstinence from fornication in Syriac-Aramaic scripture also means harlotry in general. Conscience told the Essenes that eating at the table of devils, one is communing with the fleshly body of animals in carnal lust, perhaps even worse than harlotry in one's adultery. The New Testament was founded on bloodless sacrifice, not mere ritualism. When animal flesh is assimilated by the human body, every cell of that body becomes hybrid, or rather, a mongrelized cell, reproducing bastard offspring, half-human and half-beast. Is it any wonder that Christians of Paulinism live so immorally when the best of them are of such an origin?

I do not wish to infer by the hybridization of the temple and table of God with beasts, that animals are despicable beasts, but rather that the Lord "wants mercy and not sacrifice" (Mk.9:13), let live rather than destroy, and animals are just as loveable and "good" (Gen.1:21) as any of God's creatures when living. Thru-out the Old Testament like the New, the Bible condemns vain sacrifices of flesh and blood, making void

God's commandments of not killing and eating beasts. (Isa.1:11; Acts 7:42 etc.) What I am getting at is that Paul's hybridization in communing or "fellowship with devils in pagan sacrifices", (I-Cor.10:25) as he himself calls it, is absolutely not Christian, neither is it Essene, nor of any other Jewish doctrine. The word DMA is used as "blood" (Acts 17:26), and as "bloodshed" or bleeding victims (5:28), so that Acts 15:20,29 condemns participation in the immolation or killing of animals, both bleeding the victims as the Pharisees advocated, and by strangling (to avoid condemnation of bloodshed). DeBHA means victims sacrificed, regardless if for idols or not in making the belly the god of our devotion, so abstaining from them is meat eating or killing them. Jesus complained about how the Jews have a way of making void God's word and commandments for the sake of their traditions. (Mk.7:9,13)

Furthermore, like cutting the hair, the Essenes were against mutilating any part of the body, including surgical circumcising of the foreskin, but instead taught the stopping of the fornication in humans by first giving up union with animal bodies by not eating them. "You stiff necked uncircumcised in heart and ears, you always resist the Holy Spirit." (Acts 7:51) We see here how Paul does not live by Essene interpretation of the Law, nor by his boasted Phariseeism, being a habitual law-breaker, beside a lying advocate for lawlessness.

Next, the Catholic Epistle of Jude is short, but goes straight into condemning those like the pseudo-Christian Paul. "I write and exhort you also to earnestly contend for the faith of the saints which was once delivered for the saints." This identifies him fully as a Nazarene which as a name among other things is claimed to mean to be a "contender". More, he refers to Essene scriptural history in speaking of "And Enoch also, the seventh from Adam, prophesied of these, saying, Behold, the Lord cometh with ten thousands of his saints", quoting the apocryphal Essene Book of Enoch, adding "to punish the ungodly", "These are the ones who murmur and complain, following after their own lusts, and their mouths speak flattering words, praising people for the sake of gain." Just as John warns against the deceitful fornicators and flesh eaters, such as the Nicolaitans, he traces them even to Sodom and Gomorrah. The same as John he mentions Balaam leading people to wastrel festive life, and then uses a Syriac allegory in saying, "trees whose blossoms have withered without fruit". Fruit in this case is spelled ABbA like father, but trees without father refers to harlotry, while the Tree of Life within man refers to continence, just as John says, "the seed abideth within those born of God, and lift up the serpent in the wilderness" (of lawlessness). Jude adds in 1:23, "despise even a garment which is spotted with things of the flesh." Here is reference to the immaculately pure white robe of the Essenes. People who have seminal losses or menstruation, not to speak of those abusing sex for pleasure, have a sexual smell in their perspiration, and their garments should be avoided like that of "touching a dead corpse", since it immediately arouses thoughts of lust and fornication. True apostles would not wear other people's old clothes stained with sin, since it is one thing that does not wash out. Even moreso, Jude speaks of "defiling flesh" in the Essene understanding includes "fornication with beasts", since eating animal flesh one "touches a dead corpse" violating one's Nazarite vows, becoming one or communing with a beast for sensual pleasure, instead of God. Apostle St. Jude was the founder of the first Eastern Orthodox National Church outside Jerusalem, in Edessa in 45 A.D. which became the hot bed of Nazarene Gnosticism of the primitive Anti-Nicean Patriarchs.

Returning to our exegesis of the illustrated Mystery which in the last part quotes I-John 4:1-19, in verse 9 he says: "God sent his only-begotten Son into the world that we might live thru him." So "that we might live thru him", shows our participation in the life or incarnation of the only begotten son. In other words, we live because of Jesus, the Living God, and thus Life-Giving Spirit quickens or makes us live thru him. But not all are like Jesus: So let us see if Thomism can clear this up. St. Thomas observes; "But a man thru the indwelling is called God's son by the grace of adoption. The indwelling of the Word of God is the Son of God by nature; the man in whom He dwells is the son of God by the grace of adoption. Hence, that man cannot be called "the very own" or "only begotten Son"; the Word of God alone is His own proper birth in the uniquely begotten of the Father. But the Scripture attributes the passion and death to God's very own and only begotten Son. John says (3:16) "God so loved the world as to give His only begotten son, that whosoever believeth in Him may not perish but have Life Everlasting." To this he adds: "One is said to be the son of a mother because the body is taken from her, altho the soul is not taken from her, but has an exterior source. But the body of that man was taken from the Virgin Mary."

So now we have the unveiling of the mystery that it was John who was the man or person who witnessed the incarnation of God's Word. But he is only the Son of man, while the Son of God and the Word of God are only known by the vivid presence of God experienced in the Higher Self Realization. John is not the only begotten of God, since the Presence was called by him Jesus, the Son and Word which were not born of woman, but begotten of the Father. Simon was not the only begotten, altho he experienced death and resurrection due to the Presence of Jesus. Simon was present at the virgin birth of Mary begetting Jesus, and John was present at the crucifixion of Jesus. Thomas also holds, "But a human soul and a human body constitute human nature. Thus even after the union, the human nature in Christ was other than the divinity of the Word, which is the divine nature." John and other saints are visible and tangible persons of the human form or nature, but are foreign to the divine nature, since John (I-4:12) says: "No man has seen God at any time", just as the Eastern Orthodox Church holds today as to the Son and Word of God. Man can experience Jesus Christ, just as Adam saw God walking in Paradise and John saw Jesus walking, metaphorically speaking, but the divine nature when united in nature, body, soul and will of the Word "made flesh" is said to be the Hypostasis or Person. Man does not become God, God being realized by man as the Word or Wisdom of God, similar to what the Buddha taught in the "Self-Realization of Divine Wisdom."

So St. Thomas concludes: "It is now plain that of the necessity that man was born from the Virgin Mary without natural seed." Justin Martyr puts it in another way, that the blood of the grape being the blood of Christ, it was not born of human seed. So the Lord in Syriac is written MaRIA, and thus being born of the Lord was reference to the only begotten Son, in the mystery of Virgin Birth. In the holy family there were Joseph, the foster father, Mary, the foster mother, in the human nature of those known as the Son of man, or Son of God in the divine nature, and engendered by the Mother of God in the divine; the brothers of the Lord, MaRIA, being James, Joseph, Jude and Simon. This Simon is the Zealot, who died on the Cross, being the stumbling stone of trouble, prior to his appearance in the Upper Room showing his wounds to Thomas and the Apostles, and distinct from Simon Peter known as the Living Stone of Western Church's true foundation. They all were the adopted family of Essene Nazarite celibates, or Sons of Joseph, complying with the Genesis 49 prophecies as we have explained.

John made many statements as to the living water and blood, so now he adds by saying as in this Epistle (I-5:6) which we are studying: "This is he who came by water and blood, even Jesus Christ, not by water alone, but by water and blood. And the Spirit testifies that very Spirit is the Truth." Thus, the Beloved Disciple confidentially tells us the distinguishing point of his teaching. "For this is the love of God, that we keep His Commandments. For whosoever is born of God triumphs over the world..." Believe and love Jesus, and love one another, are briefly his commandments. But he also says (I-3:9): "Whoever is born of God does not commit sin; because his seed abides in him and he cannot sin, because he is born of God." Returning to his Gospel as well as this Epistle he writes, "He who was from the beginning, the one whom we have heard and seen with our own eyes, looked upon and handled with our hands, we declare to you that he is the Word of Life." (I-1:1) To understand John, we must apply Gospel definitions, and in the beginning with him refers to what in Greek was translated as the Genesis, the first book of the Bible. So he proceeds to tell us of the Word or Wisdom of Life Everlasting, for God is Light, our true Enlightenment. Now in the 7th verse reveals: "If we live in the Light, as he is in the Light, we have fellowship with one another, and the blood of Jesus his Son cleanses us from all sins." This affirmation of John proves that the common dogmatic assertion that Jesus shed his blood on the cross in payment for our sins is false theology, hiding the Essene teachings. The blood of lambs, oxen, doves and other animals, and not even the bloodshed of humans can give us life, nor Life Everlasting. Rather, as we have already explained, the blood of the Son of God is grape blood, and Genesis teaches that the Prophesied Savior will wash his bodily raiment or robe in the blood of the grape.

John was called the Divine, that is, the Theologian, or wise in the science of divine things and God. Those who pretend that Paul, or even Thomas Aquinas were capable of usurping Theology from the true Apostle, Evangelist and Theologian, are making themselves a party with the Anti-Christ. However, if one thinks we have extended our criticism as to the interpretation that today remains in the canonical books, the Roman Catholic Church and its support of Paulinism may I quote what the Catholic Encyclopedia affirms in its own position: Volume 4 page 498 states that "it was custom of the (Christian) scribes to lengthen out here and there, harmonize passages, or to add own explanatory material." It also maintains that "It is the public character of (Christian) divines to mold and blend the sacred oracle until they comply with their own fancy, spreading them... or as a curtain closing together or drawing them back as they pleased." In Vol. 7 page 645 it states: "Even the genuine Epistles are greatly interpolated to lend weight to the personal views of the

Authors." Vol. 12 page 768 states: "There was a need for the revision (of the ancient writings), which is not yet complete, ranging from all that has been handed down from the middle ages." All this shows that the non-tampered and un-interpolated scriptures of the Essenes and Gnostic Nazarene Scriptures speaks with greater authenticity of the true primitive teachings and true Word of God than all our modern revised and censored Scriptures. Either this, or that the later divines were truer representatives of Christ than the primitive Lord Jesus Christ, which not many are willing to accept when expressed in these words.

In the viewpoint of the Roman Catholic Theology, in "Summa Contra Gentiles" St. Thomas Aquinas states: "For the Word of God and God Himself have been dwelling in all holy men since the world was founded, as the Apostle says: You are the temple of the living God, as God saith, I will dwell in them. And this indwelling for all that cannot be called the Incarnation... There must be one person of the Word of God, and another of that man who is co-adored with the Word of God... Uniquely was the union of God's Word to the flesh of Christ, marked by the Evangelist, 'The Word was made flesh'... But that man speaking of His own person, says that he descended from heaven in John, I am the living bread which came down from heaven. Necessarily then, the person and hypostasis of that man must be the person of the Word of God." From this we clearly see that John is the human person which is the hypostasis of the Word of the Living God, Jesus. Jesus is the Divine person, John is the man speaking, giving testimony on the intimate Union with God. But Thomism preaches Paulinism, thus being "all things to all people", insisting that the Son of God must die in vicarious atonement for the sins of mankind, and thus dwell in holy men thru-out time. In other words John lacks, for the Incarnation of Jesus, Simon's death on the cross and resurrection in the flesh showing his wounds to the Apostles.

According to numerous studies of bible critics, Paul's Epistles were written before the Gospels. On this supposition, in Corinthians 15:4-9 Paul affirms that Jesus "appeared to Cephas, then to the twelve; after that to more than 500 brethren at once, of whom many are still living altho some are dead. And after that he appeared to James, then to all the apostles. And last of all he appeared to me also, ignorant and imperfectly developed as I am. For I am the least of the apostles and I am not worthy to be called an apostle, because I persecuted the church of God." Here is Paul's confession of evil conscience and St. Thomas and others refer to

Paul as "The Apostle" seemingly due to his guilt making him better than the twelve true apostles. In Galatians it appears that after reproving Cephas "in his face" in Antioch, he may have been shown the scars of the crucifixion by Simon or Cephas, causing envy and the desire to prove himself as an "apostle", equal to the circumcised, for which he now claimed, "From henceforth let no man trouble me, for I bear in my body the marks of our Lord Jesus Christ." More likely than a claim for the stigmata or nail wounds, he was referring to being scourged five times, beaten three times with rods, and other protests from the disciples of John in Asia Minor beside teachings of the true apostles elsewhere. The pig-eating "Pharisee" and Nicolaitan "Gnostic" was perverting all the values esteemed by those he sought support from, and then claimed that his opponents were dividing Christ into those of Apollos (who followed John), those of Cephas (Simon Peter the Zealot), etc. beside orthodox Judaism.

The internal evidence of the New Testament unanimously illustrates, and the studies of bible critics conclude that historic evidence of a man named Jesus Christ living at his alleged time of the incarnation are non-existent. Jesus Christ is no man of mortal earthly existence, but an extra-terrestrial being promoted by the title of being the prophesied Savior of not only Old Testament Scriptures, but even of the Buddhists (Maitreya), Hindus (Kalki Avatar), Zoroastrians, etc. The Apostles' Assembly of the Essene-Nazarenes formerly confined to the Jordan, moved into Jerusalem in order to curb the contemporary hypocrisy and fallacy being preached by the orthodox Jewish doctrines. But the Epistles of Paul were written to controvert the seemingly exclusiveness of the Nazarite Essenes of possessing a risen or resurrected Savior, experienced only by their initiated seers or prophets known as the Elect. The visions and preaching of Paul were soon condemned and warned against thru-out the Mediterranean world known to be colonized by Essene followers. Paul claims to be an "apostle" for the Gentiles, but wherever he goes he seeks sympathy with the Jews with his heresies against their doctrines simply because he was born a Jew, but no longer even lived in their doctrines, and much less in the teachings of James, Peter and John in their Essene holiness. Their words had to be authenticated, showing that Jesus Christ had come in the flesh by experience. Jesus of Nazareth came to Paul rebuking him in the form of a light from the sky that shone about him, and a voice that accused him of persecution. Paul's Jesus was not in the flesh doing God's will, but rather for doing the opposite. Thus, the Jesus of Paul was that of judgement showing him to be the Anti-Christ of New

Testament scriptures. John came out frankly in his Epistles by condemning such liars who do not keep the commandments, saying everything is lawful for me. Jesus has come in the flesh only to those who really live sinless, impeccable lives knowing Him in the flesh.

Thomistic theology sought to keep the divine and human natures of the Word or Son of God together and alive, while a great deal of the criticism and commentary have sought to divide Jesus into either purely Son of God signification or Son of man, human existence, altho Jesus was well defined in the words Son of the "Living God", that is participant or practitioner of a God that is alive in one's presence, not a historic or mythic Jesus Paul taught about that came to him in an apparition. Yet in New Testament times there were men named Jesus, such as Pilate's alleged Jesus Bar-abbas, Bar-Jesus and even Bartholomew (Nathaniel) which Bar-Bahlul claimed to be the patronymic of a man named Jesus. The Evangelist and Apostle John made good his claim to having experience of Jesus Christ come in the flesh, while Paul wavers not knowing, or even caring, if his Jesus is in the flesh, with or without a body, since he also admits it was only a revelation, while he flouts the necessity of practicing His precepts to know.

So whatever the case about all the criticism and controversy as to whether Jesus lived as a human, or whether even John, or Paul and the Essene Apostles ever existed since there is a scarcity or practically no notice of Him or even the followers by contemporary historians, it really does not matter. Whoever these holy people and their description of the experience and teachings of the Savior were, the proof comes only by discerning the esoteric truth of their Word and doing the will of God in practice making Jesus Christ alive now in the Third Millennium of His Apocalyptic prediction of return. This esoteric Essene version, because of its true living substance, will fulfill the need of explaining the Heavenly Book of life, showing who were judged worthy and who remain unworthy according to their works. (Apoc.20:12) "The holocaust is at hand, beware, do penance abstaining from sin, unless you too be cast into the lake of fire like the false prophet and those who have the mark of the beast." (20:10)

I-John 1:1 to 2:1, John 6:1-15, Luke 9:13-25
WE PROCLAIM TO YOU, THAT WHICH WAS FROM THE
BEGINNING, WHICH WE HAVE HEARD, WHICH WE HAVE SEEN

WITH OUR EYES, WHICH WE HAVE LOOKED UPON, AND WHICH WE HAVE HANDLED WITH OUR HANDS, OF THE WORD OF LIFE.

FOR LIFE WAS UNVEILED AND WE HAVE SEEN IT, AND WE BEAR WITNESS AND DISSEMINATE TO YOU THAT EVERLASTING LIFE, WHICH WAS WITH THE FATHER, WHICH WAS REVEALED TO US.

THAT WHICH WE HAVE SEEN AND HEARD WE PROCLAIM UNTO YOU THAT YOU MAY ALSO HAVE COMMUNION WITH US, AND TRULY OUR COMMUNION IS WITH THE FATHER, AND WITH HIS SON, THE ANOINTED OF THE LIVING GOD.

AND THESE THINGS WE WRITE TO YOU THAT OUR JOY MAY BE PERFECT. THIS THEN IS THE GOSPEL WHICH WE HAVE HEARD FROM HIM AND DECLARE UNTO YOU, THAT GOD IS LIGHT, AND IN HIM IS NO DARKNESS AT ALL.

IF WE HAVE COMMUNION WITH HIM, AND YET LIVE IN THE DARK, WE LIE, AND DO NOT FOLLOW THE TRUTH: BUT IF WE LIVE IN THE LIGHT, AS HE IS THE LIGHT, WE HAVE COMMUNION WITH ONE ANOTHER, AND THE GRAPE BLOOD OF HIS SON OF THE LIVING GOD CLEANSES US FROM ALL SIN.

IF WE SAY THAT WE HAVE NO SIN, WE DECEIVE OURSELVES, AND THE TRUTH IS NOT IN US. IF WE CONFESS OUR SINS; HE IS FAITHFUL AND JUST TO FORGIVE OUR SINS, AND TO CLEANSE US FROM ALL UNRIGHTEOUSNESS.

IF WE SAY THAT WE HAVE NOT SINNED WE MAKE HIM A LIAR, AND HIS WORD IS NOT IN US. MY LITTLE CHILDREN, THESE THINGS I WRITE TO YOU, THAT YOU DO NOT SIN. AND IF ANY MAN SIN WE HAVE AN ADVOCATE WITH THE FATHER, THE ANOINTED OF THE LIVING GOD, THE RIGHTEOUS.

AFTER THESE THINGS JESUS WENT TO THE PORT OF THE SEA OF GALILEE, AT TIBERIAS. AND A GREAT MANY PEOPLE FOLLOWED HIM BECAUSE THEY SAW THE MIRACLES HE DID FOR THE SICK PEOPLE.

SO JESUS WENT UP TO THE MOUNTAIN AND SAT THERE WITH HIS DISCIPLES. AND THE FEAST OF THE PASSOVER OF THE JEWS WAS AT HAND. AND JESUS LIFTED UP HIS EYES, AND SAW A LARGE CROWD COMING TO HIM, AND HE SAID TO PHILIP: WHERE CAN WE BUY BREAD THAT ALL THESE MAY EAT?

HE SAID THIS ONLY TO TEST HIM, FOR HE KNEW WHAT HE WOULD DO. PHILIP SAID TO HIM, TWO HUNDRED DENARII WORTH OF FOOD WOULD NOT BE ENOUGH FOR THEM, EVEN IF EACH ONE OF THEM SHOULD TAKE A LITTLE.

ONE OF HIS DISCIPLES, ANDREW, THE BROTHER OF SIMON PETER, SAID TO HIM, THERE IS A YOUTH HERE WHO HAS BROUGHT WITH HIM FIVE FIG LOAVES AND TWO DISCIPLES; BUT WHAT ARE THESE FOR ALL OF THEM? JESUS SAID TO THEM: MAKE ALL THE PEOPLE SIT DOWN.

THERE WAS MUCH GRASS IN THE PLACE. SO THE MEN SAT DOWN, FIVE THOUSAND IN NUMBER.

JESUS ACCEPTED THE FOOD AND BLESSED IT, AND DIVIDED IT UP FOR THOSE WHO WERE SEATED, AND IN SUCH A WAY THE DISCIPLES DID AMONG THEM.

WHEN THEY WERE FILLED, HE SAID TO HIS DISCIPLES: GATHER UP THE LEFT-OVERS SO NOTHING IS LOST. AND THEY GATHERED THEM UP, AND FILLED UP TWELVE BASKETS WITH WHAT WAS LEFT OVER BY THOSE WHO ATE OF THE FIVE FIG LOAVES.

WHEN THE MEN SAW THE MIRACLE WHICH THE LIVING GOD HAD DONE, THEY SAID, THIS IS THE PROPHET WHO IS APPEARING MIRACULOUSLY IN THIS WORLD. BUT HE KNEW THEY WERE READY TO COME AND SEIZE HIM TO MAKE HIM KING, SO HE DEPARTED INTO THE HILLS ALONE.

JESUS SAID TO THEM: YOU GIVE THEM TO EAT. BUT THEY SAID, WE DO NOT HAVE MORE THAN FIVE CAROB CAKES AND TWO DISCIPLES; UNLESS WE GO AND BUY FOOD FOR ALL THESE PEOPLE.

FOR THERE WERE ABOUT FIVE THOUSAND MEN. JESUS SAID
TO THEM: MAKE THEM SIT DOWN IN GROUPS, FIFTY MEN IN
EACH GROUP. THE DISCIPLES DID SO, AND MADE THEM ALL
SIT DOWN.

AND JESUS RECEIVED THE FIVE CAROB CAKES AND TWO
DISCIPLES, AND HE LOOKED UP TO HEAVEN, AND HE BLESSED
THEM, AND DIVIDED AND GAVE THEM TO HIS DISCIPLES, TO
SET BEFORE THE PEOPLE.

AND THEY ATE AND WERE FILLED; AND THEY TOOK UP
TWELVE BASKETS OF WHAT WAS LEFT OVER.

WHILE HE PRAYED BY HIMSELF, AND HIS DISCIPLES WERE
WITH HIM HE ASKED THEM AND SAID, WHAT DO THE PEOPLE
SAY CONCERNING ME THAT I AM? THEY ANSWERED AND
SAID TO HIM: JOHN THE BAPTIST; AND OTHERS ELIJAH; AND
OTHERS THAT ONE OF THE OLD PROPHETS HAS RISEN.

HE SAID TO THEM, BUT YOU, WHAT DO YOU SAY I AM? SIMON
ANSWERED AND SAID, THE ANOINTED ONE OF GOD. BUT HE
CAUTIONED THEM AND WARNED THEM NOT TO SAY THIS TO
ANYONE.

AND HE SAID TO THEM, THE SON OF MAN MUST SUFFER A
GREAT MANY THINGS, AND HE WILL BE REJECTED BY THE
ELDERS AND THE HIGH PRIESTS AND THE SCRIBES, AND THEY
WILL KILL HIM, AND ON THE THIRD DAY HE WILL RISE.

THEN HE SAID IN THE PRESENCE OF EVERYONE HE WHO
WISHES TO COME AFTER ME, LET HIM DENY HIMSELF, AND
TAKE UP HIS BURDEN EACH DAY AND FOLLOW ME.

FOR HE WHO WISHES TO SAVE HIMSELF, WILL LOSE IT; BUT
HE WHO LOSES HIS SELF FOR MY SAKE, THE SAME SHALL
SAVE IT. FOR HOW CAN A MAN BE BENEFITED, IF HE WIN THE
WHOLE WORLD, BUT LOSE HIS LIFE OR RUIN IT.

COMMENTARY ON THE PARADISIAN ESSENE HOLY
COMMUNION OF SAINT JOHN

"There was a man sent from God whose name was John", we read in John (1:6) and again in Chapter 7:28-29, he adds: "Jesus then lifted up his voice and taught in the temple, and said, You know me and you know whence I come; and yet I have not come of my accord, but He who sent me is true, whom you do not know. But I know him, I am from Him and He sent me." This is John's explanation of why he is an apostle, or one sent from the Living God, speaking as "the Disciple whom Jesus loved".

Here we must base our conception of Jesus as an Auto-Gnosis, or the Self-Realization of the Word, or Wisdom of God: "And the Word became flesh"! The Mystery of the Incarnation is about to be clarified in this Epistle, I-John 1:1-10. As explained in John 6:51, "I am living food because I came down from the Special Presence of God", in our Syriac-Aramaic interpretation of the canonical scripture that reads: "I am the living bread because I came down from heaven." He then adds: "If any man feed on this food he shall live forever, and this food which I give is my body (flesh)." This means that living food is that which enables the realization of the Realm of the Presence of God, or being God-born he comes down from the Special Presence or the Self-Realization of knowing God, to preach this Gospel so that Heaven or Paradise may again reign on earth for the Joy of the Lord.

What I-John 1:1 describes is, "We proclaim to you, that which was from the beginning, which we have heard, which we have seen with our eyes, which we have looked upon, and which we have handled with our hands, of the Word of Life." Now, obviously John's Epistle is written to show Paul and his Nicolaitan species, with only a phantom vision of Jesus Christ, that they have not known the real Jesus. But Paul admits he does not even know whether he "knew him in a body or without a body" (II-Cor. 12:2) The meaning of this verse is that the Word of God which was spoken in the beginning or Genesis created everything, just as in the first chapter of Genesis, God said, "Let there be (whatever he willed) and it was so." That same Word of God speaks within us in our conscience if we know him, or if we really hear and obey His voice, giving us true Con-Science, meaning With-Knowledge of God. We have seen the Word of God in all His Creation with our eyes. We have looked upon and handled the Word of Life because this is what we handle in Living Food which is the body, flesh and blood of Jesus, the Holy Incarnation of His Word. The Incarnation lives in live foods.

Science has proven that heating or cooking food causes the

destruction of life in it, the vitamins and enzymes necessary for the metabolism of such food are destroyed, and in the true sense it no longer is food, a part food without life, starting the death syndrome. John fully knows the Word of Life and from experience describes it as his conception of Jesus, the Living God, as a son would, and just as your writer describes it in the return of that same source of the knowledge of the Word of Life.

"For Life was unveiled (manifest) and we have seen it, and bear witness, and disseminate (declare, proclaim) to you Life Everlasting, which was with the Father, which was revealed to us." Life Everlasting is a synonym for Salvation in Aramaic. "That you may have Communion with us, and truly our Communion is with the Father, and with His Son, the Anointed of the Living God", usually hides the identity of John's true Holy Communion with the Father and His Son, and the Holy Spirit of the Word of Life, with the use of the obscure word "fellowship". The Table Fellowship of the Essenes may have originally been a holy communion, which is called the Eucharist, and in Latin Missal, or Mass that the church supposedly celebrates by ritual, but is only mockery of the living truth. This is the Joy of Living, realizing the perfection in the living God, and the Gospel of Jesus Christ which we declare unto you, showing that God is Light, just as John was and now is a witness to the Light, and not the Light.

Then John says, "But if we live in the Light as he is Light, we have Communion with one another, and the grape blood of Jesus cleanses us from all sin." I put it in John's definition as "grape blood of Jesus" because he already has said we speak of it as in "the beginning" or headmost of the books of the Bible: "And the expected or prophesied of nations... shall wash his garments in the blood of the grape". Jesus also says, "This is my blood of the New Testament which I shed for many for the remission of sins." (Gen.49:10-11; Mt.26:28) It is the blood of the grape, the fruit juice of the vine and tree of Life that "cleanses us from all sin". This Holy Communion cleansing gives us the perfect Joy of Living in the Word of the Living God, Jesus, His Son.

When John began preaching in Syriac Aramaic, the Essene allegories unveiling the Gospel's esoteric mysteries were easy enough to come by, but in his later life among the Greek speaking people in Ephesus, etc. he had to invent a new esoteric language for the Initiates. In his own Gospel, Epistles and Apocalypse, and even in the Synoptic Gospels, the key words are defined in Greek, Latin and most other languages, and then used without warning to test how alert the disciple is in his pursuing of the true Word of God. Thus "bread" means food, as well as "to do the will of him who sent me and finish the work." (Jn.4:34) Cooking food, baking of bread, was never the will of God, since Syriac makes it alternately "hostile" as food, and the first sinners were punished losing their Paradise for the sake of eating bread in the sweat of their face, until they returned to dust of the earth.

Then Jesus has also said, "Come after me, and I will make you the fishers of men", (Mt.4:19) Obviously, if practitioners are called "the fishers of men" then the new disciples which they bring are "fishes". Up to now alternate meaning was sought by Christians in the Greek version of John, which is the word "Osparion" which can be used to mean fish, or as a delightful dish, referring directly to a submarine plant of fish flavor, really a piscine food without killing fish. It is dived for by fishermen's wives, and then made into small rissoles and partaken of with bread. The Japanese consider Osparion a delicious food; the German people to this day make it into small rolls, and inform those who inquire that it is in remembrance of Jesus' miracle of the "loaves and fishes". However, all this does not alter the use of "fishes" as "disciples" in our interpretation given above.

Moreover, Jesus uses this way of giving truer meaning to things. "These are my mother, and my brothers, those who hear the word of God and do it." (Lk.8:21) "For whoever does the will of God, is my brother and my sister and my mother." (Mk.3:35; Mt.13:50). Thus, the "loaves and fishes" are all something that does the Will of God, in the Word of God, and Jesus only considers those who do God's Will, as his obedient listeners and brothers, sisters and mother. Consequently, "fishes" are his disciples, his brothers and sisters as St. Francis of Assisi referred to them when preaching at the sea shore.

So the loaves and fishes miracle was done by feeding the five thousand with either cakes of carob meal blended with mashed bananas, or with pressed ripe fig loaves, beside the two new disciples distributing the food. However, John has no need to depend on the legends of those who heard others or saw for themselves, and so he likes to identify everybody and everything. So in John 6:9, he says "bearded figs", since bananas were also called "figs" in his time. Ordinarily, translators render it as a "bearded grain" or "barley", but wheat and rye is also bearded, or they are said to be awned. So what John means here is that among the fig leaves that his miracle fig loaves came from were with a rough surface or growth called stubble, like a man who has not shaved altho habitually doing so. He is perhaps referring to new converts who take the Nazarite vows that include not shaving or cutting the hair. Thus Adam and Eve made aprons of musa paradisiaca or sapientum (banana leaves), not the rough itchy leaves of ficus carica (fig).

To identify where he witnessed the loaves and fishes miracle, John said, (see Lamsa version): "After these things Jesus went to the port of the sea of Galilee at Tiberias," just as the Peshitta text reads. The canonical version, "went over the sea of Galilee which is that of Tiberias" is a gross error, adding four words for one letter "D" used as a preposition meaning at, of, for, to and that. What John was doing was confronting King Herod Antipas. When John wrote his Gospel he probably had seen Mark's perversion saying John the Baptist was beheaded by Herod. As explained earlier when Herodias asked for John's head on a platter, Herod ordered another prisoner's head be given to her, since he never arrested nor had John murdered, because Herod greatly admired John.

Moreover, as other critics have held, Herod Antipas built his palace on a hill at Tiberias for his headquarters of government as the tetrarch. Machaerus is an out of the way place of fearful isolation, where on its cold hilltop Salome could hardly have cared to dance naked in such treacherous surroundings, and much less would Herod have wanted to live in such a headquarters. So, on the whole it comes to a joke, since the four day journey to Machaerus from Tiberias could only produce John's head at the moment it was demanded,- had Herod in truth imprisoned him,- except by miracle. What was more probable is that Herodias was only testing Herod's manly pride, and Herod in turn playfully chides her with an Essene allegory.

To end all this nonsense, John comes marching by at the foot of Herod's marble and gold palace on the hill top at Tiberias. The climate is still like the hot trench at John's habitual hermitage at Bethany on the Jordan, Tiberias being 700 feet below sea level, and bananas, bamboo and palm trees thrive with sugar cane, overlooking the sea of Galilee. "Herod the King heard about Jesus, for his name was known to him, and he explained; John the Baptist has risen from the dead, this is why miracles are worked by him." (Mk.6:14) How else could he have cleared himself to his wife and friends, about John whom he had only beheaded allegorically, saying it was whom he had Decided to be the headmost", among the prophets. The synoptic gospels all declare: "There is no prophet among those born of woman greater than John the Baptist." Later they see John, the Hypostasis of Jesus and the big crowd go up to the mountain, possibly Mount Tabor, or others above the familiar Cana where supposedly the Disavowal of Marriage feast was held where he changed water into wine. In this vicinity the atmosphere is electrified with the spirit of miracles, and thus celebrating the Holy Communion meal on a mountain top they witness the fabulous wonder of the five fig loaves and two disciples feeding the five thousand.

For every fragment they gave away the amount was multiplied in doubling the return with which they could pay the boy for sharing in doing the will of God. Mt. Tabor, Cana, and surrounding elevations are of a cooler climate than Tiberias, so the grapes for the pressing out new wine, must or grape juice at Cana and figs thrive. Since the place on the mountain was unnamed being lonely and isolated, so that Luke 9: 10 not being an eye-witness, speculates with the guess it was a fishing port on the Sea of Galilee, which was never translated making it the town of Beth-saida, on the opposite side of the Sea of Galilee from Tiberias. John admits he went to Tiberias, walked on the Sea of Galilee and was at Capernaum, but says nothing of the miraculous catch of fish which Luke explains came about by the "Power of the Holy Spirit". The multiplication of loaves and fishes certainly was much greater than needed for "the big catch of fish" that Luke ascribes to Jesus by the Power of the Holy Spirit, while John remained tranquil at his Jordan hermitage. The John and James told of in Mark and Matthew as being fishermen partners of Simon, are all a part of a Zealot political plot, and not of John's true apostolic leadership, as we shall illustrate in volume three.

John had a definite purpose that he had to accomplish in this unique visit to Galilee when the rumor spread that John had been beheaded, and yet allegorically it explains the esoteric mystery that shows he had risen from the dead, or the plane of mortality, partaking of Everlasting Life in Jesus or the Salvation in the Oneness with God. Luke's version we have adapted to the banana and carob meal cakes and two new disciples as the true meaning of Luke's "loaves and fishes" since it is in the tropical surroundings not mentioning the mountain that John specifies in this case near Tiberias. In John 9:23, even the ordinary translations admit "boats from Tiberias, near the place where they had eaten bread when Jesus blessed it", so our version of John 6:1 is proven the true meaning.

We have the assertion of Jerome that he obtained the Aramaic original of Matthew from the Nazarenes in the fifth century to compose the Latin Vulgate version. And we have given our theory that Flavius Josephus, son of Matthew was the author of Matthew's Gospel. Going to the internal evidence in Matthew 3:4, John's food was locust pods and wild honey meaning nectarous sweet fruits. The Slav version of Josephus' writings re-affirms the same thing, while in his Autobiography Josephus tells us that in his youth he himself was a disciple of Banus, the disciple of John on the Jordan, who clothed and ate of what the wilderness provided. From the Slav version we see that this was nothing like the corpulent ox-like appearance of Thomas Aquinas, but rather like a "Spirit without substance".

In Matthew 11:7 he says, "Jesus began to speak to the people concerning John, What did you go out to the wilderness to see? A reed which is shaken by the wind?" In the Syriac Aramaic reed is written QaNIA (phonetically like the Spanish Cana), and from it comes QeNIN, QeNINA meaning substance, goods or property, so since the Greek vowel points were missing in the Palestinian Syriac of our Essene Apostles, Jerome translated substance into reed. The word RUHA means Spirit, Breath or wind. Shake is written NaD, meaning also agitate, toss or wag. So originally the Aramaic Matthew of the Nazarenes could have said John was like "substance tossed by the Spirit", instead of a reed shaken by the wind. This John 3:8 corroborates: "The wind blows where it pleases, and you hear its sound; but you know not whence it came or whether it goes; such is every man who is born of Spirit." In saying "Substance which is tossed about by the Spirit", Matthew elaborates on John's words of being tossed about like a dry leaf in the wind by one's spiritual Ecstasy or Rapture. Usually people reason about things and pull them into familiar grooves of worldly or accepted thought and beliefs, oriented by their intellectual education, which often is far from the real truth and wisdom.

Likewise, it is Josephus son of Matthew who would know why John says Jesus carried his own cross, so to justify Mark's word that it was Simon of the Quirinus tumults, he gives proof by Pilate's choice of Jesus Bar-abbas to carry the cross and be crucified. This matches well with Josephus' History of the Jews saying Simon the son of the father of the

Zealot political party was crucified. In the Catholic version Cananean is untranslated really having been TaNaNA in Aramaic, and translated as "Zealot" in all three synoptic gospels. Josephus fought against these Zealots in Galilee in trying to keep law and order in that land, unlike his experience with the peaceful Essenes.

Yet the facts he learned about John the Essene and Simon the Zealot gave him no end to botheration. Already as a youth he had thus spent three years to verify in practice scientifically that a life clothed and fed by nature in the wilderness had certain spiritual benefits and attributes of moral perfection that make spiritual powers possible. Then, also later he experimented in true laboratory style taking three expired crucified victims and with the aid of medical knowledge was able to revivify one of the three after his trauma, to live successfully. Even the story of a woman eating her own child reminded him of the gory tales told of human misery in the biblical writings. He could hardly have remained at peace without composing the History and Antiquities of the Jews in his own version that the world today honors, and last of all, the Gospel of Matthew, which unfortunately the organized Church found utile to a certain point but also subtracted much which did not suit ecclesiastical dogma. Since the mention of Jesus in his earlier writings on the Jews is out of context, it is probable that originally the words were in footnotes possibly added by Josephus himself, later placed into the text hap-hazardly even modified into meanings better suiting the fancies of the biast copyists. At least the description of the Essenes which the orthodox Old Testament ignored, and yet was made by the Church Fathers the ideal of Christian monasticism, has been duly honored by Christians.

In the third volume we shall give a collection of the sayings of Jesus from the Aramaic original of Matthew's Gospel that later became labeled as "Gnostic" and rejected by the Church, altho dear to the Nazarenes. Even in his writings on the Jews, Josephus also tells of the Essene Manahem slapping Herod in the back, or bottom, as a youth and predicting he would be a famous king, and this was carried over by Luke in composing Acts 13:1, affirming that Herod the Tetrarch was a foster brother of Manahem, and thus having the Essene training that made him highly esteem John and Jesus in their teachings.

In Luke 9:24 above we make a contextual version of what Jesus says on "denying himself and taking up his burden each day and following" Jesus. Now, the denying of self means selfless, or abnegation. However, the word NaPhShA means self, life, soul, heart, vital or animating principle. "For he who wishes to save himself, will lose it; but he who loses his self for my sake, the same shall save it." This is thus true to the gospel of Higher Self-Realization as John teaches it. Yet in the synoptic Mark, the pattern is started speaking of Simon's version of Christ losing his life to resurrect again, and thus the whole interpretation of the Gospels' and Churches' dogmatic doctrine oriented in losing life in martyrdom as the seed of sainthood.

As to "taking up one's cross", we have already inferred that it means "taking up one's Yoke", or Yoga in Eastern terminology which the Gymnosophyte Buddhists were sure to have explained to the Essenes, and obviously this means disowning one's bodily pleasures for the sake of Self-Realization of Divine Wisdom, or the Word of God within the true "Self". If we take up the meaning of crossing, yoking or bondage for the sake of Service or Ministering for Christ, the Syriac Aramaic verb EBaD means did, act, make, cross over and transgress, giving work or burden for its universal significance which herein applies to what the Buddha called Karma or evil transgressions that must be cancelled by good works. The upshot of the whole teaching is thus Selflessness, as we already illustrated in volume one as the essence of Jesus' and the Buddha's Gospel, the true and Divine Entrancement or God-Spell.

WHATSOEVER IS SOLD IN THE SHAMBLES, THAT EAT, ASKING NO QUESTION FOR CONSCIENCE SAKE: SAYETH THE ANTI-CHRIST PAUL

The Great Apostle of the Worldly Church in Rome, Paul whom, John obviously is referring to speaking of the Anti-Christ, in his letter to the Corinthians (10:25) asks men to lay aside one's conscience, and unlike the Essenes he pretends to represent in preaching Christ, participate in the devouring of fellow sentient beings. As we shall discuss in the third volume, the putting aside of conscience is done effectively by taking alcoholic beverages, smoking tobacco, opium, marijuana, and using other narcotics. People now seek freedom from moral conscience of God's Word within them, so they put their senses to sleep with drugs that deaden their contact with life, not realizing that the joy of living is realized in the plenitude of life. This is done for the sake of eating the flesh of fellow beings destroying the very Life that gives life to themselves. All Life is One and of the same origin, and the same pain they suffer from us will come back to us, and manifold since we violate the Holy Spirit of our being.

Today, cattle raising is the major cause of world hunger, pollution, deforestation and desertification. It used to be grain growing that destroyed the Gobi, Arabian, Sahara, and American deserts for the sake of bread and cereals, but today people are no longer satisfied with bread on their table, demanding steak and other flesh foods. More over with packaging of food in plastic wrappers and containers finely ground up they no longer see the four footed, winged or scaled form or hear the protest when they suffer, die and are prepared for human consumption. Today 70% of the grain produced in the United States is fed to livestock. This change from forage to feed, grass to grains has greatly worsened our ecological problems, and threatens man's survival on earth.

The converting of livestock back to totally a grass fed system in the U.S. would free up to 130 million tons of grain for direct human consumption, estimates David Pimentel of Cornell University (or much more with fruits and vegetables). This would greatly help in avoiding the 40 to 60 million deaths of mostly children among people who die from hunger and related deficiencies. The Japanese, formerly a Buddhist people are now imitating so-called American progress, in spite of having to pay 4 times as much for beef. More McDonald's hamburgers were sold in Tokyo in 1990 than in New York City. There are great ecological trends leading to a vegetarian life style in the U.S. but it is offset by a tradition of the outmoded past. This true progress is seen in the fact that from the 83 pounds of beef eaten by each person in 1975 on an average, it has fallen to less than 65 pounds eaten by each person in 1990.

The really sad part of the story is that millions of acres of undeveloped countries are used to produce feed for European livestock for export consumption. In contrast to the starving millions dying from hunger, the industrialized nations have millions dying from heart attacks, strokes, and cancer caused by eating animal flesh. According to the U.S. Surgeon General's report, 1.5 million of the 2.1 million deaths in 1987, were caused by dietary factors, including the over consumption of saturated fats. Colon cancer, the second most common form of cancer in U.S., killed 500,000 in 1990. Women who ate flesh everyday were 2.5 times more likely to have colon cancer than those who were near or strict vegetarians.

Thus, the flesh-eaters in Western countries have 10 times more colon cancer than non-beef eating nations in Asia. A Chinese study verifies that the rate of heart disease is 50 times higher in beefeating cultures than it is in countries where animal fat is still less than 1.5% of the average diet. By 1970, two thirds of the farm land in Central America was given over to the raising of cattle or livestock destined for the North American dinner table. What this cost the people is that land suitable for growing food for local people was used up by rich cattle raisers creating 35 million landless inhabitants or those with too little land to produce their own food. This then is the result of the famed Agrarian reform, showing the land was not given to the landless poor, but ended up in the hands of the rich, because the poor were enslaved with narcosis (mainly alcoholism) eating bread, rice, meat and city conveniences which they never knew when they had their own land to grow their food and were not schooled in modern forms of delinquency. Usury of the banks devalued money to buying one part of what it would buy for 133 parts its purchasing power fifty years ago.

Actually what is worse for the animal's and human consumer's health, is the feeding of cattle unnaturally on grains, growth hormones implanted in animals, antibiotics, herbicides and pesticides saturating farm lands, and even cardboard, sawdust, oil, animal sewage, etc. now mixed into their feed to reduce the cost of feeding animals. What now goes to make those yummy delicious Mac hamburgers, beefsteak and other supermarket or SHAMBLES delicacies is never to be found in fine print on the plastic container or restaurant napkin to spoil your appetite.

A study described by Pediatrics (Sept. 1989) made of 404 children raised at The Farm, a community in Summertown, Tennessee who use neither animal flesh, fish or fowl, nor milk or egg products, showed they compared well with weight and height of other children, and certainly were not filled with the causes of multiple illness mentioned above for later life. The American Dietetic Association listed the benefits of a VEGETARIAN diet in a 1988 study as being of a lower risk for coronary artery disease, colon cancer (and possibly lung and breast cancer as well), obesity, diabetes (type 2, non insulin-dependent), high blood pressure, osteoporosis, kidney stones, gallstones and the intestinal disorder diverticulosis. More on the above subjects can be found in Jeremy Rifkin's "Beyond Beef: The Rise and Fall of the Cattle Culture", and the Mar-April 1992 Utne Reader.

I-John 5:12, Apocalypse 14:18-20

WHOSOEVER BELIEVES THAT JESUS IS THE CHRIST IS BORN
OF GOD: AND EVERYONE WHO LOVES HIM WHO BEGAT HIM,
LOVES HIM ALSO WHO IS BEGOTTEN OF HIM, AND BY THIS
WE KNOW THAT WE LOVE THE CHILDREN OF GOD, WHEN WE
LOVE GOD, AND KEEP HIS COMMANDMENTS.

FOR THIS IS THE LOVE OF GOD, THAT WE KEEP HIS
COMMANDMENTS: AND HIS COMMANDMENTS ARE NOT
DIFFICULT.

FOR WHOSOEVER IS BORN OF GOD OVERCOMES THE WORLD;
AND THIS IS THE VICTORY WHICH OVERCOMES THE WORLD,
EVEN OUR FAITH. WHO IS HE THAT TRIUMPHS OVER THE
WORLD BUT HE WHO BELIEVES THAT JESUS IS THE SON OF
GOD?

THIS IS HE WHO CAME BY LIVING WATER AND GRAPE BLOOD,
EVEN JESUS CHRIST; NOT BY LIVING WATER ONLY, BUT BY
LIVING WATER AND GRAPE BLOOD.

AND THE SPIRIT TESTIFIES THAT THE VERY SPIRIT
MANIFESTS THE TRUTH. AND THERE ARE THREE TO BEAR
WITNESS, THE SPIRIT, AND THE LIVING WATER, AND THE
GRAPE BLOOD: AND THESE THREE ARE ONE.

IF WE ACCEPT THE TESTIMONY OF MEN, HOW MUCH
GREATER IS THE TESTIMONY OF GOD: FOR THIS IS THE
TESTIMONY OF GOD, WHICH HE HAS TESTIFIED OF HIS SON.
HE WHO BELIEVES ON THE SON OF GOD HAS HIS TESTIMONY
IN HIMSELF; HE WHO DOES NOT BELIEVE GOD, HAS MADE
HIM A LIAR; BECAUSE HE DOES NOT BELIEVE THE WITNESS
THAT GOD GAVE OF HIS SON.

AND THIS IS THE TESTIMONY THAT GOD HAS GIVEN TO US
ETERNAL LIFE, AND THIS LIFE IS IN HIS SON. HE WHO HAS
THE SON HAS LIFE; HE WHO DOES NOT HAVE THE SON OF
GOD DOES NOT HAVE LIFE.

THEN FROM THE ALTAR CAME ANOTHER ANGEL, WHO HAD
POWER OVER FIRE; AND CRIED WITH A LOUD VOICE TO HIM
WHO HAD THE SHARP SICKLE, SAYING, THRUST IN YOUR
SHARP SICKLE AND GATHER THE CLUSTERS OF THE
VINEYARDS OF EARTH FOR HER GRAPES ARE FULLY RIPE.

AND THE ANGEL THRUST HIS SICKLE ONTO THE EARTH, AND
GATHERED THE VINTAGE OF THE EARTH AND CAST IT INTO
THE GREAT WINEPRESS OF THE RIGHTEOUS INDIGNATION OF
GOD.

AND THE WINEPRESS WAS TRODDEN UNTIL THE GRAPE
BLOOD THEREOF BRIDLED THE BODILY PASSIONS ENTERING
IN TO BE INITIATED AND WHEN WE REAPPEARED FROM OUR
BONDAGE.

The Christological doctrines related to the Holy Trinity have caused
more blood shed for the sake of religion than any other cause. Like the
Harlot of Babylon of the Apocalypse, "In her was found the blood of
prophets and saints and all who had been slain on earth," in relation to
this church dogma. Altho I am fond of studying a great portion of St.
Thomas Aquinas's theology, but that the teachings about the Living God
be petrified and crystallized into lifeless relics fashioned like swords that
destroy the very believers and doers of His Word, dividing them in
opposite camps of battle, is far from the purpose of the doctrine based on
loving one another. Of Matthew 28:19, the only text that enjoins baptism
of Christians, "in the name of the Father, Son and Holy Spirit", we have
the ancient and weighty evidence of the father of Church History,
Eusebius, that these words are an interpolation, and instead of them, the
words "in my name" alone originally constituted that text.

Like the Catholic Encyclopedia reference we quoted earlier says,
"Even the genuine Epistles are greatly interpolated to lend weight to
personal views (of the authors)", and we might add that it was rendered
according to the views of Christian Divines, "who mold and blend the
sacred Oracles." Furthermore, the Acts of the Apostles specifically state
that the baptism should be "in the name of Jesus Christ" or of the "Lord
Jesus" four times. (2:38;8:16; 10:48; 19:5). Paul makes vague references
to baptism without specific words in four places also (Rom.6:3;Gal.3:27;
I-Cor.1:12;6:11), clearly indicating the words have gradually crept in due
to Church ritualistic dogma.

In the above text, just as it stands today in the Syriac Peshitta version we have translated, an esoteric interpretation of what John taught only to his disciples, but in turn today appears in common Bibles in the framework of orthodox Jewish indoctrination. Here an interpolation on the Holy Trinity does not appear in the Peshitta text, but in I-John 5:7 it states "And the Spirit testifies that the very Spirit manifests the Truth." In the Lamsa version this interpretation reads, "is the Truth" in place of Manifests the Truth, which he includes in 5:6, and adds the King James version of 5:7,- "For there are three that bear record in heaven, the Father, the Word and the Holy Ghost, and these three are one." Various Catholic scholars believe a similar Catholic addition is an interpolation but believe it a "needed revision". John has already testified in his Gospel, "For God is Spirit and those who worship him must worship him in Spirit and Truth." (4:24) John holds (18:37) that Jesus is the King of Truth of his Heavenly Kingdom of God. In the above text the Son referred to in the first verse comes thus: "Whosoever believes that Jesus is the Christ is born of God: And everyone who loves him that begat him, loves him also who is begotten."

As Thomas Aquinas shows, conception and birth of the Son are simultaneous. Then verse 6 seems to those whose mind is centered in theories of vicarious atonement, to refer to John's Gospel (19:34); "But one of the soldiers pierced his side with a spear, and immediately blood and water came out." But now he says, "This is he who came by water and blood, even Jesus Christ; not by water alone, but by water and blood." Since this is in reference to the only begotten, the hypostasis in the Person of John who experiences Him, not only by the Jordan water baptism, but is born again of living water and Spirit (3:5), it means the baptismal lustration of grape blood which is the water of life, or living water, scientifically excelling in vitamins and enzymes. Otto Carque has shown that grape juice is the Natural substance that most resembles human blood in minerals, and fig juice is the substance which resembles the mineral and other elements of mother's milk.

So now the interpolation of the words: "There are three who give testimony in heaven, the Father, the Word and the Holy Spirit; and the three are one," is an example of an interpolation that is non objectionable and excellent as far as John's theology is concerned. The only possible objection would be the singling out of this Holy Trinity as the only one, since there are many, just like John's affirmations elsewhere. Jesus said, "I and the Father are One, God is worshipped in Spirit and Truth, God is

Light, God is Love, the Word was God, I am the Gate, I am the Good Shepherd, I am the Resurrection and the Life, I am the Way, the Truth, I am the Living Bread cast down from Heaven and other such comparisons but God remains Ineffable. Since the Word or Logos is Wisdom, and "No man has seen God at any time", it clearly shows that the Word or Wisdom is a Spiritual Being, and thus the only begotten Son is likewise the Spiritual Presence that John speaks of saying, "In the midst of you stands one who you do not know." These people were seeking Spiritual Insight, the Divine Wisdom or the Spirit of Truth, which emanated from John's Presence, and yet "flesh and blood did not reveal it to you." Certainly not Human "blood and water"!

However, that Jesus came by the baptism of living water and grape blood (I-John 5:6) is confirmed by another Johannine interpretation in Apocalypse 14:20: "And the winepress was trodden without the city, and blood came out of the press, up to the horse bridles for a thousand and six hundred stadia." (Catholic version) This the Lamsa version interprets, "until the juice came out", instead of "blood", showing that the true meaning is "grape blood". Since the angel "gathers the clusters of the vineyards of the earth for her grapes are fully ripe", (14:18) it can only mean grape blood, must or new wine, which is grape juice in modern terminology. That this rendering of Aramaic usage is authentic without abuse of meanings is verified by the fact that George M. Lamsa, a native Assyrian, speaks and writes Aramaic as his mother tongue, having been raised among people who still speak the language that the Apostles of Christ spoke.

The bizarre and incongruent description of the visions shows that this work is the key to the esoteric interpretations of the Mysteries which the gospels present seemingly like teachings and history of the life of Jesus, and yet contradict one another. This illustration from the Apocalypse is another of many already presented to show that the "eating of the flesh and drinking of the blood of Jesus" has nothing to do with cannibalism or pagan rituals, but is used by John to teach moral ethics and dietetic principles rather the macabre and gory events of the crucifixion as our redemption obtained by sacrifice of human life or animal victims. John was an Essene, not a Pharisee.

"Then out of the altar came another angel, who had power over fire" means this angel has control, over the fire shown in the eyes of the Son of man (1:14;19:12), and since the measure of man is an angel (21:17) and the word for altar MaDBHA is the root for desert, leader and guide, beside rule dispensation or reign, it amplifies the explanation. We are thus speaking of the Heavenly Man now being realized in man's own inner Self thru the Realization experienced consciously. Now the way of inner Self-Realization of the Heavenly Man John thus reveals frankly and confidentially without allegorical mystery, since sickle MaGaLTA also means frankness or confidence, while sharp HaRIPA has alternate meaning in keen or fervent. Man must frankly be keen about the baptism of living water, by gathering in the clusters of grapes from the Lord's vineyard (Karmel or Carmel) on earth, casting them into the fruit-press, or in modern terminology their juicers. So the winepress, cider-press or juicer of wrath speaks of the Lord's righteous indignation about man's abuse to his body eating and drinking the abominable concoctions he prepares for sensual appetites, and now must undergo drastic purification with juice-therapy.

"The winepress was trodden until blood came out" refers to grape blood, which the Lamsa version translates justly as "until juice came out", renders the theme intelligible, since grape-blood is the blood that Jesus bids us to partake of for His Return to dwell in man. "Reaching the horses' bridles", is an allegory upon bridling one's passionate desires provoked by the senses in our eating and drinking, which in turn enables continence and eliminates sexual lust. If our blood is nourished by grape blood, or similar fruit juices, without seed substance we become continent virgins without sexual losses, just like children in pre-puberty youth, the true holy virginity. The size of in the winepress really is not in context to the theme or what is being taught, which should be rendered beginning or "entering to be initiated and until we reappear from our bondage." The word thousand ALPh also means beginning or entering to be initiated, while hundred MA is alternative to what, how, when or until. The word six TeSh is not even in the Peshitta text, replaced by the word METIA meaning "coming advent", or with the N suffix means "we reappear from". The word furlong or stadia ASTDA really refers to "our bondage" to our perverted sensual appetites in the above context as the alternate meaning.

This text from the Apocalypse relates directly to the beginning of the Peshitta New Testament in Chapter 3 of Matthew since the genealogy and birth legends are Western Church interpolations. John the Baptist preaches, "Repent, for the kingdom of heaven is at hand... But when he saw a great many of the Pharisees and Sadducees who were coming to be baptized, he said to them, O offspring of scorpions, who has warned you to escape from the wrath to come. Then he tells about the baptism of Holy Spirit and fire, but here we witness the Son of man in fiery righteous indignation, or "wrath" of the same Living God, that later spoke to the people of Palestine thru the Word known as Jesus, after the appearance of the great fire on the Jordan, just as the Apocalypse refers the "angel who had power over fire" and the "winepress of Wrath of God". The message is directed to the Pharisees and Sadducees, observers of rites and ceremonies of the elders, and those who denied future retribution, resurrection, existence of angels and were patronized by the wealthy, who were the opposers of the Essenes and the early Nazarene Church.

St. Augustine's view of original sin, now a church dogma, has kept a steady flow of wealth coming into the Church by way of the Sacraments beginning with Baptism to free people from the original sin, regardless what John the Baptist preached about Christ's divinity coming to him on the Jordan as an experience in Enlightenment.

That is just where "Spiritualizing Dietetics, Vitarianism", a book first published in our "Eternal Youth Life" journal 1951 to 1954, comes in. In it we honored the blessing that God gave us first, prior to man's side-tracking to error: God first consecrated fruits and vegetables that yield up their seed for the reproduction of their own species, as the God-Given food of man. When Adam and Eve questioned God's wisdom in forbidding them from eating of the tree of the knowledge of good and evil, this was contradicted by the serpent in the second chapter of Genesis. So our first point is that eating the tree which did not have fruit that yielded up its seed for propagating its own species, meant that the seed was masticated, eating the seed as its fruit contrary to God's design that the seed was for propagation. As a consequence, the seminal substance of plants overstimulated and excessively augmented human reproductive substance engendering the wild cancer-like growth of human sexual passion and population-excesses.

This dramatization of lust and related problems that divide the whole creation into opposites, is complimentary of our studies, but like Eastern Yoga doing breathing exercises to purify the effects of excessive sexual stimulation, they hope to channel libido into spiritualizing man. What we do in turn is make use of our original blessing, being created in God's image, and participating in the blessing of keeping God's Paradise on earth and eating the fruit thereof. Of course, taking steak and bread off man's table, leaving only raw salads and tree-ripened fruits, was harder for Americans to accept, but our message was far ahead of its time, waiting for the clearing of the wilderness of artificial clutter and making straight the way of the Lord in his original blessing called Paradise in the Third Millennium.

However, not by bread or food alone shall man live, even in Eden. God's blessings were not only on man and his fruit and herb diet, but there was a multiple blessing, things that God consecrated as good, wholesome and holy just as the Essenes maintained. When God created man in His image and likeness, he created them male and female, and blessed them with being able to be fruitful and multiply. In the second chapter of Genesis we have the explanation that this meant man was made to dress and keep the Garden, that is Build Paradises beside eat the fruit thereof. John (15:16) repeats this teaching saying: "Go and bring forth fruit so that your fruit remain" that is keep your Paradise producing so others may do likewise. As to multiplying, certainly the Paradises should be multiplied, but since men have sought meaning that humans should multiply, this also was to be divine. The spiritual goodness given unto man meant that he was able to reproduce bone of his bone, flesh of his flesh, by deep sleep, meaning thus what in the East is called the Samadhi trance, he could awaken other beings, materialized into being, like himself, just as both Adam and Eve, the first progeny of God were materialized. In modern times science has theorized cloning humans but were unable to go further, not having the power like Eastern Yoga Masters, who like Satya Sai Baba who currently materializes thousands of lasting material objects from the air or transformed from other things. Introductory to this is bilocation, that is being witnessed in two or more locations in the same identical moment, as your writer and others have ascertained, altho such materializations are only of momentary utility and desirability. The Hebrew Midrash explains that man originally consisted of two halves, male and female, which afterwards were separated in the Genesis legend. Male and female still have the atrophied rudimentary organs of each other, more or less hermaphoditical.

When people venture forth to become Paradisians, they want others like them to join them, and to reproduce other physical bodies that are pure in children, but instead of doing like the Son of God who did what He saw the Father do, like monkeys they aped the ape (bestial anthropoid) reproducing human flesh by bestial propagation. No longer

Gods the Father booted them out of Paradise. So-called Paradise builders only living on the physical plane reproduce only flesh of the same plane. Man should see by the present worldwide crisis that mere population explosion is man's great error, his original sin. Had he done as Jesus said, doing what He saw the Father doing, and as Adam saw God do in the first place, to plant Paradises and eat the juicy fruits thereof, and materializing his help-mates bone of his bone, flesh of his flesh, Virgin Birth would no longer remain a myth, but the very Gods would seek to live in a Paradise on earth.

True Spiritual Rebirth is also the replacing of the old man and being with the new God Person. The earth is filled with beings who would give their lives up to be made Divine, but lack the faith in themselves to live on the God-plane, naturally doing things by their spiritual potential, rather than by materialistic desire aping animals. Man's true nature needs to be humane and divine, having dominion over the beasts of earth, rather than let the tiger, the bull, pig and rat run away with his mind in mimicry. Does the animal have dominion in you?

Millions of disincarnate beings seeking higher spiritual evolution wish to incarnate and in this Third Millennium New Age will go out and produce fruit so as to keep Paradise producing, "so whatever you ask the Father in my name He may give to you". (John 15:16) So by deep prayer or meditation, even the Paradises and spiritual race of Paradisians shall inherit the earth. In the past, simplistic readers of Spiritualizing Dietetics were likely to first eat only juicy fruits from the regular supermarkets, which was wrong due to agrochemical poisoning of most food; then plant their paradises on previously poisoned land with pesticide, herbicide, or contaminated water source, wrong again; get married to someone who looks nice but is of a differing, beastly mind, hopelessly wrong; and then raise a herd of offspring who like their parents rebel to their bondage because God is really not incarnate directing their lives, or irreparably wrong since some have even voluntarily enlisted in the military, eat flesh, get drunk or do drugs, seeing no sense in childhood restrictions. Or worst of all, after a few months eating fruit, but without mentally breaking their craving for flesh-eating and sexually stimulating food, sexual life, drugs, etc. they back-slide into their same old ruts but even deeper, all because eating fruit or planting a few trees did not at all produce instant Samadhi, dirtying their hands with earth. This Spiritual birthing is not merely an earthy adventure,-the Godhood and spiritual projection into being the Heaven on earth being equally a part of it.

The Soncino Chumash explains in its illustrated translation of the Books of Moses, affirms that when Adam was told "thou shalt not eat", it was so because, "man did possess great knowledge without eating of this tree; he merely lacked knowledge of good and evil in one respect, viz. sexual passion. 'And were not ashamed': because before eating the forbidden fruit they knew not of passion, and because so far all their acts were in the service of their Maker, and not for the satisfaction of desire, consequently the act of cohabitation was as innocent as eating and drinking." Altho when one eats only fruits without partaking of seed substance, semen is not produced, yet moreover the lack of flesh and seed substance in the diet causes the return to the pre-puberty status, without curiosity nor desire for cohabitation. Even in the pre-puberty status of present civilized humans eating excessively of flesh and seeds they already often develop the curiosity and desire due to it being a secret privilege like smoking and drinking liquor as well as the built in programming of their substance in animal and seminal properties. They also translate "knowledge" as meaning "desire", rather than science. Of verse I:29 they also explain, "Thus man and beast were permitted the same diet at the Creation, man being forbidden to kill animals for food." Well,- then the Hebrew scholars, even Catholics and others, claim God's law was changed by the Flood. Anyone with a conscience like the Essenes knows this is false, since there is an abundance of food for everyone on our earth if the human population ate no animal flesh, since even eating all the grains fed to fatten animals for meat, would easily feed the whole of human population, and more, if used for vegetables and fruits on the same amount of land as used to grow grains.

On pages 65-66 in our first volume, "Unveiling the Gospel's Divine Mysteries", another Hebrew scholar reputed as the greatest authority on spiritual revelations of the Bible, radically unveils some of the mysteries about Genesis. He would destroy a paradise of fruitful trees saying "trees" should be translated growth or growing. The tree of knowing good and evil, he translates "good" TOB to mean beneficent, cheer, joy or mirth; and "evil" RA to mean life-giving, so we have a "Knowing growth of life-giving joy". Next Landone interprets "serpent" NACHASH as Divine Experience or God Power, and beguiled NASHA to mean lifted up, so that Eve said: "Divine Experience has lifted me up," and God said: "Behold man has become one of us." Having this God Power, however, we would interpret simultaneously with the innocent joy of mankind, ADAM, enjoying Paradisian fruits as food and planting more paradises from their seeds, as truly the knowing of the Divine

Inspiration of Godhood, as Co-Creators.

John's interpretation of Genesis must have been identical since he says as "Moses lifted up the serpent in the wilderness so must the Son of man be lifted up," Of the original progeny of God, Eve said, "Divine Experience has lifted me up," eating whatever she did that gave her "knowing of the growth of life giving joy", which thus proves Dr. Landone's interpretation makes all the trees of Paradise identical; that is, the tree of life and the tree of knowing the growth of life giving joy!

For several thousand years, man has been immersed in sin and sorrow, because the truth of Paradise was not allowed to be experienced by men. "In the sweat of your face shall you eat bread," and "Every moving thing that is alive shall be food for you, only the blood thereof you shall not eat," (Gen.3:19; 9:3,4) according to John, the Nazarites and the Essenes, are the work of men remaking God's laws to eat what they want and not what God wills or designed for his happiness. By returning to God-Given food man's life would return to prepuberty youth of an ever-virginal consciousness, freeing itself from the possessiveness of worldly objects, wealth and their cares, releasing in him the inner joy of communion with the source of Illumination and Wisdom in the Word of God.

Now, we have inferred that when God made man in his image and likeness, male and female, meaning according to John's Essene definition, that it was in the likeness of Spirit and Truth. Moreover, it is the Spirit that "quickeneth" or makes live, while the flesh profits nothing. In Genesis, likeness is written DEMUTH, which according to Landone means "capable of assimilating and manifesting God". As with John, by making live or quickening here we have God manifesting in projection, that is loving, as the God action. As to the nature of this likeness of God as Spirit in man, this has to be experienced in practice to be known, making Jesus, the Living God a living realization. In 1939 after only a year eating strictly juicy fruit, with a companion your writer was levitated physically in the Florida everglades to a distant location, consciously feeling the descent from the air near a highway in meditative prayer. However, we were studying about Yogis doing likewise and practicing exercises to achieve it. Your writer has also told of his experience in bilocation, in which physically he was inactive at home, but those who greatly desired my activity with them, saw my body materialized with them, leaving a church, eating bananas at a farm festivity, walking on water on Lake Quilotoa, and so forth. When I tell these witnesses that I had not gone away from my hermitage, they become distressed because they had seen me do otherwise.

This likeness is not like the things on the plane of opposites, good or evil like the tree of knowledge or desire, but made and blessed by the Spirit of Truth. Moreover, this is male and female, or the androgynous spiritual man as the likeness and mold or "image of God". As we have just described, this androgynous spiritual man can be known by others in materializations of bilocational or multilocational experience where man reproduces or multiplies his own species by spiritual projection. In another occasion your writer appeared in the hut of an Indian family one evening, healing a child who had been crippled for years, all of which was contrary to his habitual life as a hermit, illustrating the powers coming of Divine Will rather than personal effort in sending forth love and good will to all beings.

As we have explained in the first volume, John's androgynous spiritual person, or Jesus, was experienced walking on the Sea of Galilee, healing, preaching and even feeding thousands of admirers all over Palestine without John needing to travel away from his hermitage.

However, in the third chapter of Genesis, it says the Serpent was more spiritual than any of the other creatures that God had made, since the word "subtle" can only mean less material or spiritual. In turn, Matthew tells of Jesus teaching, "Be wise as Serpents, harmless as doves", meaning Jesus is in accord with the interpretation of the Serpent as a source of spiritual wisdom. Eve wondered why the Lord God, Adonay Elohim, had said that they must not touch or eat of the tree of knowing good and evil. In the Hebrew translation of Soncino Chumash it even intimates that the Genesis 3:4 words, "You shall not surely die", meant that the serpent pushed her on to the tree and said to her, as you did not die from touching it, so shall you not die from eating thereof. In verse 6 it adds: "And when the woman saw the tree was good for food, and was a delight to her eyes, and the tree was to be desired to make one wise, she took the fruit thereof and did eat; and she gave unto her husband with her, and they did eat. And their eyes were opened..." The Lamsa version and similarly the Catholic Bibles translate it as "the tree was delightful to look at", while the Hebrew Soncino and King James versions agree it should be "the tree was to be desired to make one wise".

In summary, "to make one wise" means capable of feeling or experiencing pleasure and pain, that is, only by experiencing do we know that with every pleasure of earthly existence there is a binding and corresponding pain for a consequential equilibrium, manifesting God's Presence everywhere, without any place to hide. The only escape is rightly partaking freely of Living Water, from the Tree of Life Everlasting. When Adonay Elohim asked Eve, why she had eaten what was forbidden, she said; "Divine Experience has lifted me up;" and the Elohim, meaning Gods said, "Behold man has become one of us, to know good and evil, and now lest he put forth his hand and partake also of the Tree of Life, and eat, and live forever" and drove man out.

Now in all of this we see that subtle spiritual man can exist as part of earthly existence, as the writer experienced in levitation, or apart from the body as others witnessed in bilocation. Jesus was capable of being witnessed in the bodies of his Apostles, and other times was seen, heard, tasted or touched, and then dematerialized back to pure Spirit. Feeling or sensibility, seeing, hearing, tasting and touching, are the 4 rivers that flow out of man's Garden of Eden or pleasure within the physical body. Knowing of this Tree means the desiring of the fruits of good and evil, just as Jesus said "By their fruits shall you know them." But John insists that to know Jesus come in the flesh, we must abide in Him, keep His commandments, so His Living Water and grape blood will cleanse us from sin. Thus, Jesus in us no longer fears the "flaming sword which turns every way, to guard the path to the Tree of Life" (Gen.3:24) since "Perfect love casts out fear...He who fears is not made perfect in love." (I-Jn.4:5)

Eating of the Serpent's or Naas tree, that is the nut or seed tree will not make one wise and in youth it overwhelms the body's reproductive potentiality forming evil habits in wasting sexual substance and energy. Like the Sons of Seth who lived on apricots, figs, grapes, and other juicy fruits one can live like "Sons of God", as the most holy and righteous tribe that ever lived. Yet when they began partaking of almonds, apricot kernels and other seeds and finally bread made from grains in the plains where the children of Cain dwelt, they too replaced their bodily Garden of Eden guided by the Word of God, with a place of torment guided by Satan. The Serpent shows the Way to Wisdom, the Word of God, or the Way to Error, the worldly foolishness of Satanic bondage. The Book of Adam and Eve tells how they were restored to their higher status by listening to the Word of God. However, after acquiring Divine

Experience, making them wise, once having eaten of the forbidden Naas tree, their bodies no longer were androgynous and spiritual in substance, but now they acquired "garments of skin to clothe their (spiritual) body", forever reminding them of the Paradisian Garden of fruit, but overcome by the downflow of the four rivers they would soon end in the sea of death, (Dead Sea) like the Jordan. The short-sighted translators bound to their anthropomorphism make God into a tanner and tailor of animal skins when the true meaning is "clothed them with (human) skin".

In turn, as to clothing of fig leaves, this the Talmud says were of the tree "wherewith they had sinned, they also made amendment." However, figs are a juicy fruit whose seeds neither are assimilable, nor can they reproduce their kind, so they cannot be of the Naas tree, the tree of Sin and Sainthood, Good and Evil. Moreover verse 3:8 says: "Man and his wife hid themselves from the Presence of God among the trees of the Garden," meaning they were hiding the evidence of sin, and fig leaves were something that would surely betray them since they were forbidden to even touch the tree of knowledge or desire.

Still another viewpoint was expressed by science in classifying various species of bananas, which ancient legend claimed to be the fig of Paradise, since ordinary fig leaves are unsuitable for garments due to the itchiness produced by a digestive enzyme in them similar to the papain in papayas, while banana leaves are easily made into skirts or cord in an emergency. The familiar commercial banana is of the "musa sapientum" species, and the more plantain flavored variety or pinkish flesh is that of "musa paradisiaca", meaning respectively "fruit of the wise men" and "fruit of paradise". It originated in India.

Nevertheless, in the Book of Adam and Eve, it says that Seth and his children dwelt on the mountain below the Garden (of Paradise), meaning Mount Hermon, reaching 9,000 feet altitude, where only the true fig (ficus) grows on the lower slopes, being too cold and high for bananas. This text even claimed that figs were the size of watermelons showing the soil to be much more fertile in their time. The proof of this came when they became aware that "the lord God clothed them with skin", due to the itching irritation of such fig leaf skirts. Adonay Elohim thus foresaw man's shortsighted tendency to transgression thus making the innocent-appearing clothing, potential "hair shirts" of penitential design, reminding the sinners that figs are God-Given food and not meant to clothe those who were "naked and not ashamed"!

Pursuing the banana idea and ideal of Paradise further, the "fruit of the wise men" and the "fruit of Paradise" types of bananas grow plentifully at Jericho, and thus at "Bethany" near the Jordan Crossing (Jn.1:28) which are over a thousand feet below sea level, accounting for the tropical climate. Thus "Bethany" probably was not of true fig garden signification, but rather it meant "banana grove or plantation". This "Bethany" location of John's Gospel would tally with the synoptic gospel's mention of John's food being "locust fruit and wild honey" meaning "carob and bananas and other sweet fruits" as we inferred in volume one. In the present incarnation your writer again eats carob meal with bananas from his Bethany paradise at Shambhala Sanctuary just as John had at his Jordan hermitage. Bananas do fairly around the Sea of Galilee, 682 feet below sea level, and certainly no bananas can grow at the mistaken modern location of Bethany opposite Jerusalem on the Mount of Olives, revealing the story of Jesus cursing the fig tree to be a myopic fib on the part of the translators. It instead shows Jesus' knowledge of fruit growing, in that planting a "fig" or banana tree at such a high altitude with killing frost is an error, sin or curse in translation. That it withered losing its leaves was not due to Jesus, but wrong site. Jerusalem is 2,500 feet above sea level, the Mount of Olives being slightly higher, which is not much less than 4,000 feet above the level of the Dead Sea measured at 1,290 feet below ordinary sea level. However in the gorge below Jerusalem at Gethsemani, which means olive oil press, olives do grow meaning possibly figs also, but up on opposite side on the Mount of Olives at what is called Bethphage, named so for error of planting bananas where they could not properly ripen. From our experience at Shambhala we find that figs will grow but lack soil fertility to produce well in our tropical highlands, but bananas do much better as the case with Jericho.

So, returning to Eden, God did not clothe man in animal skins, but rather gave man extremely sensitive human skin. It is always man who invents all kinds of paraphernalia to undo God's intentions, and then blame their anthromorphistic God. Satan inspired the children of Cain to invent trumpets, horns, string instruments, cymbals, flutes and sundry instruments to play sweet music that ravish the heart, to ferment alcoholic beverages and establish taverns, to make gorgeous apparel dyed crimson and diverse colors in many patterns, exhibit horse racing and finally go to war against one another in progressive ability to kill, with their claim to romantic chivalry and making life easier for men with added knowledge. To speak of holiness and saintly lives today is to portray a life of strictness in morals and discipline with no adventure and pleasure, when in reality those who persevere in the religious life know of more Divine Joy and freedom than those bound to painful slavery to the few paltry pleasures in worldly life, soon to be concluded in pain, aging and death.

Now we have affirmed that "Eating of the Serpent's or Naas tree, that is, the nut and seed tree will only make one wise in old age, but in youth it overwhelms the body's reproductive potentiality forming evil habits in wasting sexual substances and energy." This means that once one has established dominion in complete continence for years, then if one eats seed substance or cultured dairy products, one may find sometimes that "Divine Experience has uplifted me," momentarily. This happened to Adam and Eve as mentioned earlier, but only robbed them of their wonderful and fructiferous Garden, but they repented and the Word of God had mercy on them. In the case of your writer and Gautama Buddha, it was the eating of clabber or curds that brought deep Samadhi experience. Thus, Yoga also advises milk and fruits and other light foods to purify the body, but when one is well established in continence and other disciplines for years, they advise partaking of heavier food like the Buddha did. With the aging of the body more protein is not needed for physical or spiritual development, using nuts, seeds, sprouts, curds, etc., which in earlier manhood or womanhood would thwart their dominion of continence.

To illustrate this, after the writer's 7 month 7 day fast on 99% pure tinctured water, eating fruit and baked potatoes, he obtained the greatest strength he ever had physically, beside the greatest weight, from 135 lbs. to 212 lbs. due to the multiplication of greater digestive assimilability achieved in only 4 and one half months, before starting another 6 months 17 day fast of similar type. The food eaten after a prolonged scarcity naturally is economically utilized, altho it may not give the spiritual faculties and greater powers ordinarily, except in the case when one has lived strictly on juicy fruits and succulent herbs, like Adam and Eve beside their son Seth, or the Buddha living on wild fruits, jujube and fasting for 7 years, when he partook of curds. Most people who try fasting, fruit eating or other abstinence for months or years, have not and are not prepared in their spiritual attainment and dominion, and thus return to eating by overdoing and destroying any progress they have had. Divine Experience does not come from mere sensual satisfaction.

In summary, one must remember John's words in the Apocalypse (22:14,16,17,18,19): "Blessed are they who keep my instructions that they may have a right to the Tree Of Life, and may enter thru the gates of the City. I, Jesus, have sent my angel to testify to you in the (Essene) churches I am the root and offspring of Adam, and the bright and morning star. And the Spirit and the Bride say Come. Let him who hears, say Come. And he who is thirsty, let him come. And whosoever will, let him take of the Living Water freely. I testify to every man who hears the words of the prophecy of this book, If any man shall add to these things, God shall add to him the plagues that are written in this book: And if any man take away from the words of the book of this prophecy, God shall take away his portion from the Tree of Life, and out of the holy City, and from the things which are written in this book." Here John warns the interpolating Divines of their fate in Karmic works that will rebound just as we now witness at the beginning of the Third Millennium of the Christian Era. We have outlined his Essene criteria and pin pointed the main errors.

In the above quotation, "root and offspring of David" as today translated is a weird falsification of John's text, just before he warns the falsifiers of their consequences. Neither Jesus nor John have any Davidic lineage, or want to be associated with the things King David did. John has been talking all along of the Tree of Life and living water, which relate to Adam in Genesis, which is the true Son of God heritage. The ancient Armenian version reads "root and offspring of Adam", as is worthy of the Divine Origin of the Son of God, and not murdering military leader whose moral example caused his son (Solomon) to continue with a vast concubinage and proliferous harem of wives and offspring. The Heavenly City that John speaks of describes the pure river living water gushing out of the throne of God and Prophesied (Lamb), "In the midst of great lane of the City, and on either side of the river, was the Tree of Life, which bore the twelve kinds of fruits, and each month it yielded one kind of fruit; and the leaves of the trees were for the healing of the people."

What better message could be prophesied for the Camp of the Saints in this Third Millennium? However, the condition is that we keep the Essene Jesus' instructions or commandments: Build Paradises and eat the fruits thereof.

IN RETROSPECTIVE EPILOGUE

In this second volume of "The Buddhist Essene Gospel of Jesus", altho the subject matter changes in its exposition, we still continue Unveiling the Gospel's Divine Mysteries, now especially as to the Esoteric Essene Allegorical Jesus Christ incarnate in the flesh. At the end of the first century, John was able to make sweeping changes in the coming equivocal trends creeping into the Gospel of Jesus, that separated the political Messiah and the Antichrist into opposing camps to the Camp of Saints led by John.

First came the Davidic lineage that was promoted to bar John from Messiahship, which he truly did not want ever on his own part. His Messiah was an omnipresent Christ incarnate and partaken of in everyday common food and drink in those who overcome flesh and blood desires. In his First Epistle (1:7; 5:6) John says his Gospel needed none of Davidic genealogy of a political warrior, which were later interpolated to support political conquests, with only "a word to the wise which is sufficient". "This is he (Jesus) who came by (living) water and (grape) blood, even Jesus Christ; not by water only, but by water and blood." "And the Spirit testifies that that very Spirit is the Truth." In the beginning Genesis (49:11) we are told the blood of the grape shall cleanse the garment or body of Expected or Prophesied One, and Jesus says his blood is the blood of the grape. Moreover, the Apocalypse also confirms, "These are those who came out of the great tribulation, and have washed their robes and made them white in the blood of the Lamb;" "For the Lamb shall lead them to fountains of Living Water." (7:14,17) And the Lamb is the Light of those who are saved (21:24) so thus we know this is Jesus, since in Aramaic AeMRA means Lamb, beside being derived from AeMR and AeMIRA, the predicted, foretold or prophesied. So when John sees Jesus walking by at Bethany on the Jordan, he said "Behold, the Lamb of God."

However, John has no controversy about "I need to be baptized by you" (Mt.3:13) or "When all the people were baptized, Jesus also was baptized" (Lk.3:21). John saw Jesus, the Son of the Living God, walking, just as Adam and Eve heard the voice of God walking in the garden, and he who sent him to baptize with water, said, "The one upon whom you see the Spirit descending and resting, he is the one who will baptize with the Holy Spirit." (Jn.1:33) The Spirit rested on Jesus like a dove, so henceforth John and John's disciples follow this spiritual guidance of

Jesus, just as Adam and Eve followed the Elohim. So immediately this spiritual Jesus says, "If a man is not born of (living) water and the (Holy) Spirit, he cannot enter into the Presence of God." In brief, as Justin Martyr confirms, the Christ has blood, but not of human seed, having Divine virtues. This is because the blood of the grape does not beget men, but God, so the Scripture has shown that Christ did not come from human genealogy, but by divine virtue. Only political warrior Messiahs or kings need Davidic lineage. Because the blood of grapes and other fruits are up to 90% living water with vitamins and enzymes, the Salvation of Jesus, requires a lustration with living water and the Spirit to know the Presence of God. There is no water tossed on crying babies or childish adults after one understands John, without preconceptions from those who surely were not eye-witnesses, but fabricated mythical gospels on legends of the past.

Yet while Christians hid in the Catacombs under Rome, rather than be sacrificed to wild beasts for the cruel sport of the opulent rulers, the earliest symbol for Christ Jesus was the two fishes, of the loaves and "fishes" miracle. Fishes were new disciples caught by the fishers of men. Tertullian elaborated on this: "We little fishes follow the example of our Ixthus (Fish) Jesus Christ, are born in the water, nor otherwise than abiding in water, are in the state of salvation". Thus, the Roman Church gained acceptance in the fourth century without any picturing of a man crucified for anthropomorphistic worship of a dead god who awoke from his drunken stupor the third day. The Greek word Ixthus is an anagram for Jesus Xristus Theou Uios Soter, or Jesus Christ, God's Son, Savior. Jesus is thus a "Fish",-Ixthus!

It was not until the Council of Constantinople in 707 that the picture of Jesus Christ was ordered to be drawn in the form of a man: in place of a figure of the lamb, used at that time, there was to be a figure of a man nailed to a cross. In Christian art the earliest instance of the crucifixion of Jesus Christ thus appeared only in the eighth and ninth centuries, according to Mrs. Jameson in her "History of our Lord in Art". The same affirms, the figures are with the body upright, arms extended straight with no nails, no wounds, no crown of thorns, frequently clothed with a regal crown, a God, young and beautiful. There was no compulsion or pain shown, since the doctrine of vicarious atonement of Jesus met with no success with the Jews, for they regarded a man that was crucified as a great curse. (Deut.21:23) Thus, it proves Christianity from the beginning made its inroads into the Roman Empire and eventually the whole world thru the beauty of the Sermon on the Mount, John's mystical theology and the bloodless sacrifice of Jesus Christ incarnate in the Holy Communion of Christians.

But with the publication of the Latin Vulgate in the fifth or sixth centuries, and the removal of the mystical esoteric allegorical symbology in portraying the Son of the Living God, into a political human symbol of bloodshed, it was made over into a tool for the political Zealots of the Holy Roman Empire persecuting the Cathars, Albigineses, the Moors, the Jews, Luther and Calvin Evangelistic theology, etc. losing the original character of the Essene Daily Communion to be shared as Jesus returned in the incarnation of his flesh and blood. Instead of the Messianic return in the repast of Christians, the pious feast on fellow sentient beings, cooked condimented and salted grains with alcoholic beverages, if not more potent narcotics.

This past Era from which all history is dated as the Piscean Age began with the junction of Saturn and Jupiter in the sign of Pisces, which became Christian with the birth of Ixthus (Christ the Fisher). There are drawings of fishes seen in Roman Catacombs. With our teaching unveiling the Living Water in Grape Blood, fruits and vegetables as our Living Food descended from Heaven as the true Salvation in the Paradisian New Age otherwise known as the Aquarian Age of the living water man, John the Baptist and Apostle unveiling the God Spell of the Son of Living God, speaks again the Good News.

OUR GARDEN OF EDEN FINDINGS
AND VITARIAN CONCLUSIONS

The Gnostics, Dr. Landone and other learned scholars, like Eve were not so bright after all, because by translating the eating of the Tree of Knowledge had caused Eve to say "Divine Experience has exalted me", they still admit Garden of Eden means Envelopment in Desire. Yet other Hebrew scholars of Soncino Chumash show Knowledge also means "Desire", DAATH, similar to EDEN, or "Pleasure" or "Desire". So our original 1954 thesis, "Spiritualizing Dietetics, Vitarianism", is vindicated in that eating of nuts, seeds or seminal substance is what gave man and woman sexual desire and the cause of degeneration.

Likewise the Buddha acknowledged that Desire was at the root of man's suffering in Samsara of worldly Karma. While I have warned young people that eating of NAAS, Serpent's Tree of Desire in seed substances causing the wasting away of the life substance of the body, in later years seeds etc. do not give seminal losses and women come to their menopause. However, in reality this is not so much the dominion of sexual desire, but rather the result of an accelerated aging process, the degeneration and disintegration of our carnal Envelopment of Desire, or bodily Garden of Desire.

Dr. Johannes Rutgers, M.D., the Dutch advocate of Birth Control, wrote: "The essential constituent of seminal fluid is the microscopic sperm cells harvest of an embryonic tumor. Even in regards this discharge, the reproductive cells occupy a position intermediate between the increase of growth on the one hand and the tumors of age on the other hand." He blamed excessive eating of an albuminous nature as the cause of sexual stimulation, just as we point to albuminous seed foods, beside animal products.

So in reality, due to man's subdued will to live and wasted youth, in later life we need to refrain from seminal and protein excesses for health. Observe that mother's milk, in an infant's greatest increase of growth period only contains 1.6 % protein, so nature intended only fruits and vegetables low in protein as man's food. Yet, animal flesh, cheese, nuts, are ten times excessive, peanuts, wheat germ, soybeans, etc. being extremely excessive. As shown in our Modern Live Juice Therapy, the use of vegetable and fruit juices, or what Jesus called Living Water, heals all kinds of disease and retards old age. Your editor likewise found that eating seed proteins, altho giving an exalting euphoria of forbidden food, is like habit forming narcotics, leads to rapid aging and death. Just as the Hebrew word for Tree means "growth" also, The Tree of Desire is really fostering evil "growths" of age, tumors, adipose flesh, irritating uric acid of rheumatic ailments, etc. Our correspondents William Goodell and Dr. Zinn of Canary Is. have found men in India with ages over 1,000 years living on fruits high in living water, just like Adam learned to do.

"Behold man has become one of us, to know good and evil, so lest he put forth his hand and take of the Tree of life, and live forever," God made man work building his own Paradises and eating fruits thereof.

APPENDIX

DIET OF THE ESSENE JESUS

Josephus, the renowned historian who lived during the first century, says John lived on carob, eating neither bread of any kind nor the flesh of animals, beside refusing wine and intoxicating beverages. But the Gospels now read John the Baptist ate "locusts and wild honey". The Locust tree and fruit are carob, otherwise known as "St. John's Bread" or food, because Luke (7:33) says he ate no bread. However, the words "wild honey" the Hebrew scholars in the Soncino Chumash translate as "fruits that exude sweet juices", such as "dates and figs". This would also include the sweet grape which yields a delicious juice when freshly pressed. In the Holy Land many fruits abound in many varied micro-climates including; grape, fig, dates, banana, carob, mango, peach, apple, melon and citrus.

THE HEALING TRANSITION DIET

The Healing Transition Diet, based upon the Mucusless Diet Healing System of Professor Arnold Ehret and re-discovered by Diego Conesa from Cartagena, Spain detoxifies the body gently to avoid overwhelming the eliminative organs allowing one to slowly adapt to the fruit diet of the Essene prophet. Arnold Ehret; "In this very important lesson it is necessary for me to convince you, once and for all, of the following facts: First--that in food (in diet) lies 99.99% of the causes of all diseases and imperfect health of any kind." The transition diet is begun eating twice a day, for lunch and dinner, a raw salad of lettuce, spinach, grated carrot, tomato and sauerkraut dressed with fat, protein, plus steamed vegetables and a cooked starchy food. The amount of mucus being eliminated by the body is artfully controlled by the amount of cooked vegetables and mucus forming food eaten.

Cooked starches like brown rice, potato and rye crisp bread (Wasa, Ryvita etc.) are mucus forming while steamed starchy vegetables such as broccoli, cauliflower, cabbage, eggplant, string beans and squash are non mucus forming but help slow down the elimination. Steamed vegetables and steamed apple can be eaten with the salad, starch is eaten last to ease digestion. Protein is in the form of either mayonnaise; made from two eggs with olive oil (refined/virgin type is tastier than extra virgin for making mayonnaise) slowly added while blending, add sea salt OR raw clabber; made by keeping raw milk at room temperature until curdled. You can use just the whey, which has most of the minerals, by filtering the curds from the whey using a mesh colander or you can use a mix of the curds and whey. The cream can be scrapped off the top with a little added back for flavor if desired. The recommended fats to use are olive oil, a little avocado and olives. Olives help neutralize acidic toxic matter. These concentrated proteins and fats are all mucus forming and thus one needs to wean oneself off of eating these foods very gradually over time, thereby avoiding severe withdrawal reactions like; nervousness, weight-loss and weakness. If your elimination is speeded up, one needs to balance it out by eating more cooked and mucus forming foods and even add extra meals sufficient to reduce the speed of your elimination.

Season the with olive oil and a little herbal sea salt. Steamed eggplant or cabbage topped with steamed tomatoes makes a pizza-lasagna type dish. By eating only twice a day you are fasting most of the morning and at night on vegetable or fruit juice, lemonade or herb tea. Heat treated bottled juices are good being less cleansing than fresh juices, but also good are fresh vegetable juices like a carrot, spinach, celery, parsley mix. When you have been on the transition for a while and are sufficiently detoxed, fasting can be started; 24-36 hours or longer as can be tolerated without cleansing too fast using lightly sweetened (agave nectar or stevia drops are recommended) lemonade (made from pure water) or vegetable or fruit juice or just water. Short fasts aid the detoxification process. Breaking a fast on a raw salad is needed for beginners, due to their high toxicity, to avoid danger (people have died breaking fasts on dates or cooked potatoes) but those advanced on the transition can use juicy fruit. Laxatives, like senna tea, taken at the beginning of a fast will empty the bowels which makes fasting a lot more pleasant. For longer fasts (3, 4, 5 or more days) a laxative taken right before it ends helps clean out toxins that have accumulated during the fast. For beginners a colonic administered by a professional or a high enema are a great help in removing hardened mucus that forms on the walls of the colon from years of not eating right.

When cleansing too fast the face becomes drawn, the hair turns grey, arm and leg muscles shrink, the energy level drops and you get depressed. If this happens the key is to eat enough; cooked vegetables like broccoli, protein and fat, and if needed brown rice to slow down the rate of elimination. The vegetables provide fiber to scrub the long alimentary track and sponge up excess mucus. Beginners in the transition will need (in order of most to least mucus forming): whole grain pasta, brown rice, potatoes and rye crisp bread to slow down the elimination of high levels of waste products in the body. We are much more toxic than our predecessors due to accumulative degeneration and thus need a long term adaptation. The laxative quality of each meal is important, avoiding constipation and intestinal bloating. A move toward naturally grown, chemical free foods is recommended, avoiding contaminating the body with agricultural poisons. Emotional flare-ups, nervousness and headaches are usually caused by a failure to eat on time of the right, agro-chemical free foods which will stop the elimination process and supply blood sugar. A complex vegetable meal with protein, fat and starch will stop your elimination and make you feel great. There is a rhythmic schedule to the meal times. You will begin to feel a little less centered or stable as soon as you start cleansing too much or are lacking blood sugar, occurring 3-6 hours from the last meal. Over-exercising, over-working and excess stress can also speed up the elimination. Vegetable juice and wheatgrass are good supplements. Avoid indigestion by eating only when the stomach is empty, not over eating, eating when relaxed and watching food combinations

Protecting your teeth is very important; making sure you clean them after every meal by flossing, rinsing with a mouthwash or baking soda and then brushing with a good toothbrush and toothpaste. Avoid green pineapples or any fruit that is not sweet smelling and ripe. Unripe citrus is a problem for the teeth because it drains minerals to counteract its acidity. If you cleanse too fast (i.e. you don't eat enough cooked vegetables, protein and fats, and you eat too much fruit) your body will become acidic and this in turn will draw on the mineral reserves of your teeth and bones to nuetralize the acidity. Mineral rich carob pods and carob powder mixed with bananas will help your teeth stay healthy. Clabbered or cultured milk (yogurt, cottage cheese, whey) has calcium and other minerals to help the teeth. If you cannot tolerate the high protein and fat of whole yogurt or raw cheese (which will occur as you become cleaner) use just the whey liquid. Vegetable juice extracted fresh with a juicer is a good mineral source. Cucumber, spinach, lettuce, celery, carrot, tomato, bell pepper, parsley, cilantro with a little lemon juice added for flavor, makes an excellent vegetable cocktail. Nori flakes and kelp powder or granules (Maine Coast Sea Vegetables have good products) are good mineral supplements and are the best way to salt your food. By avoiding cleansing too fast and by ingesting carob, cultured milk, raw vegetable juices and sea vegetables you can be sure that your teeth, bones and nerves will stay healthy.

The Healing Transition is a long process (Professor Ehret took about 8 years to completely detoxify his body) to offset the many years (20, 30, 40 or more) of eating incorrectly thus patience, faith and courage are needed to stick with it all the way through. Professor Ehret's books, especially The Mucusless Diet Healing System, explain this diet further. Very gradually one eats less mucus forming foods, enabling a smooth, relatively stress free transition. Cooked broccoli and cauliflower are mucusless but slow down the rate of elimination as do cooked fruits like apple. First one starts eating cooked starch like brown rice or potato twice a day after the vegetables, then after some years only once a day, then later no starch is included, but always striving to eat just two big meals a day (occasional fruit breakfasts/afternoon snacks are ok if needed to keep your energy up so you can work normally).

After some years one can eat cooked fruit for the first meal and salad with cooked vegetables for dinner. Salads at this stage can be dressed with just olive oil, sauerkraut, lemon, seasoned rice or apple cider vinegar, eliminating the protein. Olive oil is a better fat than avocado at this advanced stage. Olive oil is lighter and easier to wean oneself off of than avocado. Olives are still eaten. Cooked fruit ideas are; steamed apple slices mashed with cinnamon/whole sugar, dates/dried figs (steamed) and stewed prunes. Cooked fruit compote can be made with mashed banana and other fruits. Very slowly and gradually add more raw fruit until fully adapted to raw fruit. Thus, you will be eating just raw fruit for one meal and a salad with cooked vegetables (squash is good at this stage) for the second meal. In your selection of raw fruit avoid excessive, cleansing citrus or pineapple (especially unripe, acidic fruit) which will speed up your elimination excessively. Carob powder mashed with banana is delicious and high in minerals. Eventually you can give up the cooked vegetables and just eat a raw fruit meal for lunch and a raw salad meal at dinner, with juice taken in the morning. Very gradually reduce your olive oil and olive intake.

An ideal, mucusless, fruit only diet requires special conditions like mineral rich, tree ripened fruit from your own garden and a low stress, natural lifestyle living in the country or suburbs with a warm, dry, sub-tropical climate. If you have the conditions necessary you can drink juice in the morning and eat raw fruit at both meals for one day per week at first (the other days you are eating raw fruit for lunch and a raw salad for dinner), then slowly add more days of just fruit until you adapt to an all fruit diet. You may choose to drink juice (fruit juice ideally and vegetable juice when needed) in the morning, eat solid fruit at lunch and take juice at night or you may need two solid fruit meals per day, whatever suits your body the best. Or you may need to stay on a low mucus forming vegan diet, if you lack the ideal conditions needed to live exclusively on fruits, taking juice in the morning, sweet, non fatty fruit for lunch, and for dinner a salad made from starchless vegetables (lettuce, spinach, celery) and botanic fruits (bell pepper, cucumber and tomato) with cooked starchy vegetables as desired (broccoli, squash etc.) dressed with olive oil, olives, lemon juice, seasoned rice or apple cider vinegar for dinner. For the morning juice one could start with a glass of orange-mandarin juice, followed by a glass of pineapple juice and then a have a vegetable juice cocktail. Remember the success of Professor Arnold Ehret in achieving a high level of health using the mucusless diet healing system principles.

Made in the USA
Middletown, DE
21 September 2021

48672552R00064